Holy Places

Holy Places

MATCHING SACRED SPACE
WITH MISSION AND MESSAGE

Nancy DeMott, Tim Shapiro, and Brent Bill

THE
ALBAN
INSTITUTE
Herndon, Virginia
www.alban.org

The Alban Institute
2121 Cooperative Way, Suite 100
Herndon, VA 20171

Unless otherwise indicated, Scripture quotations are taken from the New Revised Standard Version of the Bible, copyright 1989, Division of Christian Education of the National Council of the Churches of Christ in the United States of America. Used by permission. All rights reserved.

Information in appendices is taken from the Indianapolis Center for Congregations' Using Resources series and is available in PDF format at www.centerfor-congregations.org.

Cover design by Spark Design, LLC.

Back cover photo by Jane Mastin.

Library of Congress Cataloging-in-Publication Data

DeMott, Nancy.
 Holy places : matching sacred space with mission and message / Nancy DeMott, Tim Shapiro, and Brent Bill.
    p. cm.
 Includes bibliographical references.
 ISBN 978-1-56699-345-6
 1. Church. I. Shapiro, Tim. II. Bill, J. Brent, 1951- III. Title.

BV600.3.D46 2007
254'.7—dc22
                              2007031221

        12   11   10   09   08   07   VG   1   2   3   4   5   6

To the congregations who faithfully participated in the Indianapolis Center for Congregations' Sacred Space Grants Initiative.

gratis

Contents

Appendices

Acknowledgments

While our names grace the cover of this book, the work that led to its publication involved the efforts of many people. First, we want to acknowledge the resource consulting work of the entire Indianapolis Center for Congregations staff, as well as their various levels of participation in the Sacred Space Grants Initiative (SSGI). We especially thank Jerri Kinder for her work on this manuscript.

Next, we want to recognize our educational design partners. Their wise counsel and work helped us put together a program and process that was meaningful and helpful to the SSGI participant congregations. Our partners were Jerry Cripps of InterDesign, Tuomi Forrest and Robert Jaeger of Partners for Sacred Places, Jon Pahl of the Lutheran Theological Seminary at Philadelphia and author of *Shopping Malls and Other Sacred Spaces*, and Kevin Ford of TAG. Tuomi and Bob of Partners for Sacred Spaces, along with Buzz Reed of Klein and Associates, also served as helpful readers of drafts of this book.

Then come our congregational coaches: Glen Bell, Ced Cox, Clarence Crain, Nicole Floyd, Ivan Douglas Hicks, Peggy McDonald, Sherry Perkins, and Susan Weber. These were the folks who worked directly with congregations, taking the information from the class sessions and making it specific and applicable to each congregation.

We were fortunate to find people who had the unique combined skill sets of experience with congregations and caring about sacred spaces.

We also appreciate the fine work of the Alban Institute and its publishing department. Richard Bass, Kristy Pullen, and others helped us take our vision for this book and put it into words that congregations across the nation will find helpful.

Finally, we need to thank the Lilly Endowment. The endowment enthusiastically supported SSGI and made it possible by generously funding the work.

Introduction

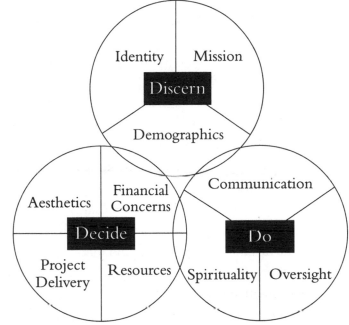

*B*uildings communicate. Stained-glass windows, high altars, multipurpose worship-gymnasium spaces, Plexiglas pulpits, padded pews—all these and other architectural elements say something about a congregation's theology and mission. They point to a faith community's beliefs about worship, identity, purpose, and more. From the stark simplicity of a Quaker meetinghouse to the splendor of a Romanesque revival building, sacred spaces speak loudly. What they say can either reinforce a congregation's mission or detract from it.

The purpose of this book is to help congregational leaders—from expert builders to novices—hear what their buildings are saying and then learn how to implement a process we call the *sacred space model* to ensure that the building communicates the message they want it to convey. Each phase of the model—discern, decide, and do—consists of a series of questions that a congregation must address.

The book is designed to be used by congregations that are contemplating or are involved in work on their facilities. This could include renovation, remodeling, expansion, or building. Our unique *discern, decide, and do model*, coupled with a sacred space team, assumes no particular level of prior knowledge about building issues to be successful. The book is intended to help you develop your sacred space team, create a reflective approach to your work, enable you to learn from one another, and make space for discerning God's direction for your congregation. It is effective because the model begins with congregations where they are and helps them move to their next desired level. After working with more than three hundred congregations through our consulting and innovative Sacred Space Initiative,[1] we know from experience that it is a process your congregation can use effectively.

Let's take the sacred space team idea first. What is a sacred space team, and how is it any different from any other committee or project team? First, it is not a collection of building experts. Rather, it is a group of five to seven people charged with determining what your congregation wants to do in relation to a building project. Second, a sacred space team works by enlisting the ideas and support of all aspects of a congregation as it works on building issues. It also builds wide congregational support. It gets many stakeholders involved. That way any project becomes more than just one person's, or group's, idea. A final benefit is that, when done well, it elicits congregational members' undiscovered talents.

So how many people do you need on a sacred space team? It is important that the team be limited to five to seven members who are open-minded and objective. Team members also need to be committed to giving the time and energy required for a process that may last up to three years. They must be leaders who have a vision for the congregation. A diversity of ages and of length of time in the congregation is also helpful. Persons who have construction experience may or may not be appropriate for the committee. That is because construction knowledge is not the most important criteria for team members. Instead, team members need to possess wide general knowledge.

While it is tempting to think that the sacred space team needs to represent every ministry area in the congregation, such an approach often makes the team too large for effective decision making. To ensure the needs of ministry areas are heard, name a subcommittee of representatives who are appointed for the express purpose of providing input from their ministry areas. How you decide who is key depends on your congregation's culture and method of operation.

Once you have established a sacred space team, this book will help you learn how to implement the discern, decide, and do model. As we said earlier, you will learn how to ask important questions. The *discern* phase of the model focuses on *who* questions. Who are we as a congregation (identity)? Who are our neighbors (demographics)? Who is God calling us to be (mission)?

The *decide* phase of the model concentrates on *what* questions. These questions concern the types of decisions you will need to make in any size building project. The four questions used by the model are representative, not comprehensive: What do we want our building to convey (aesthetics)? What approach to building will we use (project delivery)? What service providers will we use (resources)? What sources of funding will we use? (financial concerns)?

The *do* phase of the model centers around the implementation phase(s) of the building project. As in the other two phases, the questions are representative, not necessarily comprehensive. They are *how* questions. How will we keep the congregation informed (communication)? How will we maintain our spiritual focus (spirituality)? How will we ensure that the work is done properly? (oversight).

The book will show you the processes behind each question and introduce you to real congregations that have used this model, and you will be able to see how it worked for them. We will give you practical help, in both process and resources, to meet the challenges of your sacred space project, no matter how large or small.

Another purpose of this book is to help you think about how your building is used and what changes could be made to make it more useful. We will provide you with options for building stewardship or expansion and help you determine how your building team can work with a governing board and the rest of the congregation.

We will also prepare you to think through the dynamics that may occur within a congregation during building or renovation. We will give you guidance in helping your congregation function through the implementation of sacred space–related plans and in working your plan in a way that frees the rest of the leadership so they can continue key ministries.

Sacred space teams may use this book in a variety of ways. Your team may read the entire book and then begin to work your way through it. Or you may read a section or a chapter and bring it to a team meeting for discussion. We have included summaries of each chapter for easy access in team meetings. We have also developed a list of vital questions for each chapter that you can use in team meetings. You will find helpful charts, surveys, and other resources for your team included in the appendices. Everything about this book was designed to allow you to use it in the most helpful way possible for your situation. Our hope is that each congregation that uses this book will be empowered, in their own distinctive way, to improve or expand their use of their sacred space.

Architect Rudolf Schwarz said, "It is only out of sacred reality that sacred buildings can grow . . . . That sacred substance out of which churches can be built must be alive and real to us."[2] May this book contribute to your congregation having a sacred space that is alive and real to you.

PART 1
DISCERN

CHAPTER 1 Who Are We as a
Congregation?

Identity

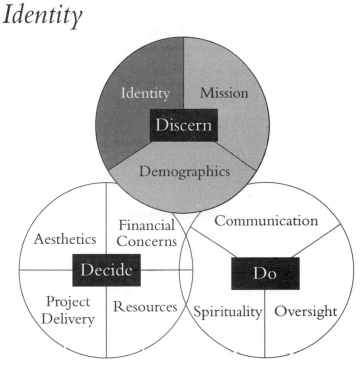

$\mathcal{A}$ pastor of a large congregation is talking at a ministerial association breakfast. "Our building scares people," he says. The listener wants to know more. "Well," says the pastor, "we are a large cathedral, and when people walk in, they feel so small. At one time our cathedral might have been comforting to people, but now it's just scary." He goes on to say that his congregation wants to make their space a warmer, friendlier space. "It's one thing to have an imposing sanctuary," the pastor says, "it's another to be known as an imposing congregation."

This wise pastor grasps what is obvious but often unstated— every congregation has an identity. This identity is communicated by collective characteristics that are recognized by others. These collective characteristics can include such things as style of worship and ways of greeting strangers. A congregation's identity, whether acknowledged or not, shapes its decisions and behavior in the same way that an individual's genetic and social identity affects his or her behavior. Congregations that understand and can accurately describe their identity are in a better place to act on their strengths than congregations that cannot.

Every congregation is unique. Each has their own identity. No faith community is, or should be, an exact clone of another. In the book of Revelation, John of Patmos, at Jesus's command, writes decrees to seven churches. Actually, each edict is written to the "angel of the church." These angels are heavenly representatives of these seven faith communities. They also represent the distinct identity of each congregation. The angel of the congregation in Ephesus is patient. The angel in Smyrna is long-suffering. Pergamum's angel is faithful. We might use some of those same words to describe our own congregations. We could say that one congregation is "alive" while another is "prayerful." Or one is "contemporary" and another is "traditional." In doing so, we, like John of old, understand that individual faith communities have their own look and feel. Each is distinctive.

Many aspects of our life together say who we are and what matters most to us. How a congregation worships not only communicates beliefs about God but communicates self-understanding too. Rites of passage, such as baptisms, bar mitzvahs, and first communions, are key indicators of a congregation's character. The ways a congregation celebrates birth, observes initiation, and supports the dying are indicators of their core identity. Another way of understanding a congregation's identity is to see how they eat together. Is the meal formal or informal? Who goes through the line first? Who sits where?

Or one might listen carefully to how congregation members talk about their clergy. Is she or he called a pastor? A priest? A preacher? Something else? The language we use to describe clergy is often an indicator of our congregation's identity.

It is easy to see how a congregation's awareness of their identity affects decisions about their building. One downtown congregation that we know states that their mission is to "share God's grand grace with the local community." When this congregation remodeled their sanctuary, they had the architect design a clear glass window behind the pulpit. That way, on Sunday, worshipers stay focused on the town they serve, which is visible through the new window. The sanctuary design thus reinforces the stated identity of the congregation.

Your Building Speaks

Actually, all buildings speak, and they speak in many ways. Sometimes they use written words. Drive through the Midwest and you see barns proclaiming, "See Rock City," urging travelers to visit a massive natural rock formation atop Lookout Mountain in Tennessee. Sometimes buildings speak out loud. In the center of Indianapolis, when you walk past a radio station's building, you hear what is currently on the air. Other buildings speak without words. An elementary school that shines with faculty and students working together has walls that whisper, "These children are special." Some older adults live in homes packed with memories that sing, "Don't leave." Visitors to the Holocaust Museum in Washington, D.C., note that the walls there ask people to become quiet and reverent.

In Annie Dillard's book *Teaching a Stone to Talk*, she tells of a man named Larry who lives with a palm-sized stone that he is trying to teach to talk. Dillard isn't clear what it is that Larry is trying to teach this stone to say, but she is clear that Larry is serious about the endeavor. Whether Larry knows it or not, he is tied to an ancient tradition that says structures—stones and bricks and locations—speak. They may not use words like humans do, but they do communicate meaning related to the events and experiences associated with them. [1]

We see this illustrated in the Genesis account of Jacob running from his brother, Esau. Jacob lived for some time with his uncle Laban, a shepherd who had two daughters, Rachel and Leah, both of whom Jacob married. Jacob agreed to work for Laban for seven years in return for the right to marry his daughter Rachel, and because of Laban's trickery in substituting Leah as Jacob's bride, Jacob ended up working another seven years. When after all of these years of hard labor Jacob decided to leave with his wives, children, and herds to establish his own household, Laban became angry and chased after him. When he caught up with Jacob, they made peace. As a sign of this covenant of peace, Jacob set up a stone as a pillar. Soon the relatives gathered more stones to complete the memorial site, and they broke bread together there. The stones in this place spoke. They witnessed to the promise that Jacob and Laban would do no harm to one another. The stones spoke the word *peace*. [2]

This biblical account and others remind us that the buildings housing our congregations communicate. Even if the people themselves are silent, whether in prayer or in doubt, the stones cannot be silent.

Two books that describe the experience of listening to the language of congregational buildings are *The Geometry of Love* by Margaret Visser and *How to Read a Church* by Richard Taylor. In *The Geometry of Love*, Visser takes the reader on a tour of St. Agnes Church near Rome. The book describes the meaning, symbolic and functional, of many aspects of the building, including the altar, the nave, and the narthex. In a way, the book answers one of the key questions asked above: "What about our facility leads people to deeper practices of faith?" While the book focuses on the beliefs of the Roman Catholic tradition, its form of study is applicable to many faith traditions.[3]

How to Read a Church is appropriate for those who are part of a liturgical Christian community. In this book, Richard Taylor describes and interprets symbols and images found in many Lutheran and Episcopal buildings. For instance, he describes how to read the meaning expressed by particular crosses and crucifixes, as well as the meaning behind particular words and letters carved in stone. He ends the book with a chapter on how to "read" the clergy leader and the congregation itself.[4]

Many other books are available that those of other faith traditions may find helpful (see appendix G). These books help us see that congregations meeting in buildings that express beauty and faith through symbols and design tell stories about how their facilities reinforce their faith identities.

In the 1600s the clergy-poet George Herbert argued that a religious building should be read as a text. Herbert noted that for the church building to be read that way, it should contain an abundance of Scripture in various places.[5] While that may not be appropriate for your tradition and congregational culture, Herbert does help us think about how to read a building. One way to look for the message that a religious building communicates is to interpret the building in the same way one interprets Scripture. This looking includes seeing what the whole facility has to say. Discerning the meaning of Scripture includes looking at the history, the form, the context of the writing in relation to what is around it, what it does, what it intends, and the reader's response to the passage. Discerning a building includes these same actions. Ask questions. What is the history of this sacred space? How did it come to this place? What does the shape of the building say? What do people do here? How do people respond to this room? What does our sacred space keep people from doing?

Sacred Space

You may have noticed that when we say "sacred space," we mean the whole building, not just the sanctuary or part of the worship area. That is because we believe that a sacred space is any part of a building used by a congregation or for programs hosted by a congregation. The term "sacred space" is not meant to confer a particular aesthetic or assume a particular theological perspective. Those are congregationally determined. The process, the resources, and the tools we describe can be applied to any aspect of matching a congregation's physical structures with its goals and dreams. A congregational team may want to learn what their sanctuary communicates, or they may be trying to understand how their parking lot communicates the positive core of a community's way of life. All aspects of a facility communicate, not just the obviously sacred ones. Even functional ones like parking lots and kitchens reinforce or fail to reinforce a congregation's intentions.

Understanding congregational identity is essential to a building program. As your sacred space team works on building issues, you need to discern what is unique about your faith community. You also will want to think about how your facility communicates that uniqueness. The primary goal of discernment is to be more conscious about how the building effectively communicates your congregation's distinctive identity.

Listening to Your Building

There are a variety of ways your sacred space team might discern your congregational identity by listening to your building. One way to discover the link between your congregation's identity and your facility involves asking two key questions: "What about our facility leads people to deeper practices of faith?" and "What about our facility drives everyone crazy?" The answer to the first question shows where the congregation's identity and facility come together in positive, faith-giving ways. The answer to the second question shows where gaps exist between the congregation's identity and facility. These two questions are starting places for exploring the relationship between mission and building.

Another way to learn what your building communicates is to talk with those who experience the space. Every congregation has building stories. For example, a sacred space team working on building issues in a medium-sized Presbyterian congregation discovered stories about lights going out in the sanctuary, a plan to plant flowers along the sidewalk, and the successful effort to put up a new sign near the road. These stories were new to many of the team and gave them a deeper appreciation of the other members' emotional investment in their building.

One way of getting at your congregation's stories is to convene a group of about twenty-five people (though this conversation can be adapted for smaller or larger gatherings, based on the size of your congregation). The twenty-five then break into groups of two to four people. Each small group is asked to come up with a story about your congregation's facility. The small group needs to agree on the story and assign a storyteller who presents the story to the entire group. The story needs to be specifically about an event in which the facility is the main character. The story should take no longer than one minute. Tell the groups to be succinct and to remember that stories start in one place, then something happens, and finally they end in a new situation. Some tension or conflict needs to be at least partially resolved.

When this process was used in the Presbyterian church mentioned above, participants discovered that almost every group told some version of the same story. This was their "big" story. That story, with slight variants, went like this:

Many of you will remember this. It happened when we moved from downtown. The sanctuary was finished, so was the education wing. We needed one thing to complete the project. The last task was to place a steeple on top of the sanctuary roof. We wanted it tall, beautiful, and visible from far away. In addition, we wanted the placement of the steeple to be an event—not just any event, but a sacred exhibition. We hired a helicopter to fly the steeple in and literally drop it on the roof. The press was there along with the local television anchors, and there was a live radio broadcast. We were passing out brochures and offering refreshments. It was spectacular. Perhaps a bit too spectacular! Just as those in the helicopter were ready to let go of the steeple and pass it to those on the roof, the pilot lost control and the helicopter spun around. The cross crashed to the ground and split to pieces. Miraculously, the helicopter did not crash and no one was injured outside of a minor bruise or two. We made front-page news, and the wire services picked up the story. Twenty years later, we still have no steeple.

In other congregations, the "big story" won't be quite this dramatic, but it's likely that the groups will focus on a similar theme.

After the stories are heard, ask the group to think about these events. "What common themes did you hear in our stories?" "How would you describe the character of our building in the stories?" "What is our building trying to tell us through these stories?" You can also ask the two key questions named earlier: "What about our facility leads people to deeper practices of faith?" and "What about our facility drives everyone crazy?"

In the example of the Presbyterian church's crashing steeple, the answers reflected spiritual discernment about the mission of the congregation and the configuration of their sacred space. Some of their comments were:

> In this experience, the building taught us not to reach too big or too high.
> You can be faithful without being spectacular.
> It was our up-close-and-personal temptation narrative.
> We are a congregation that likes excitement. Maybe too much.
> Pride goeth before a fall.
> Our lives teach us to embody the way of the cross; the building itself doesn't need to.

Using conversations like this helps a sacred space team discern ways their building matches their identity. Such conversations help people own, or discard, common stories about the facility and the mission it supports. They are a way to interpret the experiences people have with the facility.

Interpreting stories about their building does not tell a group what to do. Discernment involving a shared story does not furnish a group with an architectural design for a new community room or an elevator. Thinking together about such stories does, however, help congregations consider who they are and how their building shapes their character. It is one of the first steps for effective improvements to a sacred space. It also needs to be part of an ongoing discipline of discernment that shapes the sacred space process.

Another way a congregation can discern how its building communicates its identity is to take members on a building tour. Tours are not just for historic cathedrals! This exercise works best in a small group, like that of a sacred space team. The group takes a walking tour of their facility. At each room or space, the group stops and responds to these questions:

- What goes on here?
- How does this space help or hinder the activity?
- What is the best thing about this space?

Another way to do this without actually walking through the facility is to have people draw the building's floor plan on poster boards. Then ask the above questions and write the answers in the appropriate spots on the floor plan.

Both of these exercises allow the building to tell the story of its usage. They are ways for the building to describe capacity issues, identify strengths, express the needs of upkeep, and demonstrate evidence of wear and tear. They encourage members to examine congruencies and gaps in what their building communicates in relationship to the congregation's personality.

When a sacred space team from a Baptist congregation sketched their floor plan, a communal shout of affirmation rose. In unison they shouted, "It's the basement; see, everything is influenced by the basement!" By looking at the whole facility, the group was able to see how problems related to their basement (too much moisture) were keeping them from moving ahead with other aspects of their ministry. This was a congregation wanting to be a beacon in their part of the city, and they were stuck underground.

Taking a close look at what their building was saying led Etz Chaim, a synagogue on the north side of Indianapolis, to a whole new place. In the early part of the last century, some Jews from Greece settled in Indiana. They were part of the Sephardic tradition, Jews originally expelled from Spain. There aren't many Sephardic communities left in the United States, and this congregation wanted to make sure their children understood the richness of their tradition.

The facility where they gathered was a former Lutheran church. As the years passed, Etz Chaim had to address structural issues related to the building. While working on major maintenance issues, the sacred space team decided to think bigger. Etz Chaim wanted more than a repaired old Protestant building; they wanted a space that communicated their unique cultural, historic, and religious identity to the generations to come. Thus, they chose to build an entirely new building on a new site.

One way their new building communicates their identity is through the placement of the ark that holds the Torahs. When this community prays, they want to be praying east toward Jerusalem. In their old building, they had to face north. Now, in their new facility, all face east, toward the ark, toward the Torahs, toward Jerusalem.

They also have a new kosher kitchen. They are, as one member says, "a social congregation." Now they are able to host gatherings in which the food prepared and served on site is kosher.

For Etz Chaim, building a new facility that matched their identity didn't mean leaving everything behind. Just as they brought their traditions with them when they came to the United States, when they moved, they brought things from the old building, including several stained-glass windows, the ark, and the Torahs. They didn't wipe away the past. They added a new chapter to an identity that stretches back in time and now, thanks to the new building, continues into the future too.

Listening Objectively

Listening to what your facility is saying requires objective distance. It is easier to make assessments about the identity of communities to which we don't belong. We need to be able to be as unbiased about our own congregation as we are with other congregations. Think of a congregation where leaders say, "We love our youth" but put the youth room in the basement boiler room. It is hard to see such a discrepancy without stepping back and viewing it from some distance.

That is partly because a building becomes part of us, like a good pair of tennis shoes. It is comfortable, so we often miss things the building is trying to tell us. We never notice that the front door slams too hard (not very hospitable) or that the nursery is too cold (parents who are longtime members bring extra blankets, but visitors don't know to do this).

Such things can lead to a gap between a congregation's stated identity and its functional identity. A congregation may call itself "the fellowship that reaches out," but if people in the community know the doors to the building are locked all day, the message rings false. What they say doesn't match the reality of what they do. Comparing our building to our beliefs can help ensure congruency between what we say and what we do.

Some sacred space teams find it helpful to interview recent visitors and ask them questions about the building. This allows the building to speak through the experience of those who might see things differently and is also a way for those working on sacred space issues to view their work through the eyes of the larger community, not just longtime members. A good way to do this is to ask three to six new members or recent visitors the same set of questions about the facility. These questions should be open-ended. Ask questions that you and your team do not know the answers to. Following are some sample questions you may want to adapt for your use:

> When you drove by our building for the first time, what did
>   you think?
> What is kept up well?
> What looks messy or in disrepair?
> What stories have people told you about our building?
> What part of our building feels familiar to you and your un-
>   derstanding of a congregation?
> What part of our building feels strange to you and your under-
>   standing of a congregation?

Many of us are familiar with the old hymn about the church in the wildwood. Some leaders from a rural congregation told us that visitors and new members said that when they drove by this church building the first time, they thought of that song. Each visitor affirmed the rural character of the setting and the way in which the building and grounds allowed for lingering on a Sunday morning. So, when this congregation began designing a new education wing, they already knew that gathering space was a high value and that the new building should disrupt as little of the surroundings as possible. They knew they had succeeded when, after construction was complete, they had much more space and were still referred to as the little brown church in the vale.

People often think of building projects as knocking out walls and putting up new ones, as activity filled with sweat and swinging hammers. Essentially, though, good projects begin with the mind. Discernment is perceiving accurately with the intellect, detecting patterns and comprehending what is distinct. Listening to what a building has to say helps you to see where your facility stands in relationship to what you want to accomplish as a congregation. Sacred space teams that begin with discernment and build discernment into every phase of the project are more likely to adapt or construct facilities that are true to their congregation's mission.

Your building has important things to say. And who better to listen than those who care about its message?

Summary for the Team

- As a congregation's sacred space team works on building issues, it needs to discern what is unique about their faith community. Does the building communicate the congregation's unique identity effectively?
- All aspects of a facility communicate. Even more functional aspects, such as parking lots and kitchens, reinforce or fail to reinforce the congregation's intentions.
- Sacred space teams that begin with discernment and build discernment into every phase of the project are more likely to adapt or construct facilities that are true to the congregation's mission.
- Sometimes there is a gap between a congregation's stated identity and its functional identity as expressed by the facility. Becoming more conscious of these gaps is a goal of discernment in a building project.

Questions for the Team

1. Who, outside your usual conversation partners, do you need to talk to in order to get an objective view of what your building communicates?
2. What stories have people told about your building?

3. What about your facility leads people to deeper practices of faith?
4. What about your facility drives everyone crazy?
5. How will your sacred space team weave elements of discernment into the rest of the phases of the program?

CHAPTER 2 Who Are Our Neighbors?
Demographics

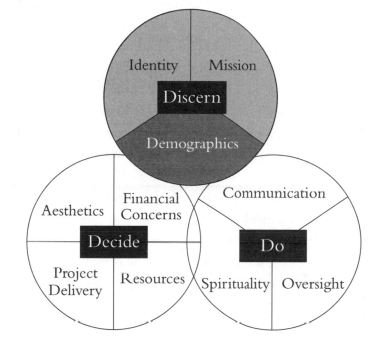

*I*magine discovering a huge number of young families in your congregation's neighborhood. That's what a small congregation in our program found after doing a demographic study as a part of their sacred space discernment process. They were surprised to learn that there had been significant growth in the number of young families living within a five-mile radius of their location. This caused them to reflect on and discuss what the implications of this information were for their congregation. As a result of that news and their discussion, they designed a new nursery space so that young families who visited could be confident that their children were safe and well cared for by the church.

Demographic information also influenced a large congregation situated among the cornfields about five or six miles from a growing community. They learned that the purchaser of some adjacent farmland intended to build eight hundred new homes that would surround the church. Though not a shovel of dirt has been turned, the congregation is already discussing and planning how this new influx of neighbors will impact their ministry and eventually their facilities.

These two stories remind us that congregations do not operate in isolation. They affect and are affected by their neighbors. A congregation's relationship with its neighbors influences its identity and its decisions about its facilities.

That is why the second part of the "discern" phase of the sacred space model asks, "Who are our neighbors?" For a congregation to discern what God calls it to be in its particular context in a particular time, it must understand the community in which it serves. Our sacred space model calls this step "demographics."

Demographics

Demographics are "the characteristics of human populations and population segments."[1] Discerning the demographics—learning and understanding the characteristics of your community, your neighborhood, and your congregation—is an important part of the discernment process that informs your building project.

Without a clear understanding of your neighborhood's makeup, your congregation may be offering ministries and programming that don't relate to the needs of those nearby. Kevin Ford, chief visionary officer of TAG, a consulting organization that helps congregations and businesses with market research, demographic studies, and strategic planning, tells of a congregation in the suburbs of a major U.S. city that tried to reach young adults ages twenty-five to thirty-five. In spite of all their efforts, they failed to do so. They hired Kevin to do some market research in hopes that new information would enable them to reach the young adult population. What Kevin discovered was that the congregation was located in an area filled with young retirees. They moved there to get away from the hustle and bustle of the city and to own some acreage. The nearest significant population of young adults was ten miles away, closer to shopping malls and restaurants. Kevin told the congregation that if they wanted to reach young adults, they needed to relocate. They stayed where they were. Then Kevin led them through a strategic planning process during which they realigned their ministry to meet the needs of the young retirees geographically close to them.[2]

This story is an example of why demographics are important in the discernment phase of congregational facility planning. Data about the community and the people who live there enable a congregation to fine-tune and/or realign their mission. Mission impacts facilities. Sometimes congregations die as a result of waiting too long to look at and understand what is happening around them. Many urban congregations find that those they were founded to serve—such as Irish or German immigrants or downtown businesspeople—have migrated to other parts of the city. They now go to other places of worship. We know of a congregation that has worshiped for 132 years in the same building. They are in a region that has seen economic depression and population decline. Their worship attendance has dwindled to forty-five, and they try to maintain a building that has long been too big. They feel stuck. The repairs on the building strap them financially. There is no economic development in the surrounding area. That means it is unlikely that they will be able to sell the building and begin worshiping elsewhere. They can't afford to tear down the building. Insurance to cover their liability if they vacate would be burdensome. They don't know what to do, so they do nothing. Could an examination of the economic and population trends fifteen to twenty years ago have prompted a different decision about their oversized building? Perhaps so.

Demographic data and community trends that are used to shape a congregation's focus can make a significant difference. How does your congregation find this vital information? The good news is that a wealth of demographic data is available to congregations. Much of it is free. There is so much of it, though, that it often seems a daunting task to collect and make sense of it. To help you think about what demographic information will be most useful to your congregation, we have divided the kinds of data into three broad categories: (1) information about people who live in the geographical area in which your congregation is interested, (2) information about community trends, and (3) information about those currently participating in your congregation. A description of each of these kinds of information follows, along with tips about where to access the information.

Geographical Boundaries

Before we get into an exploration of the three categories of data though, we need to say a word about geographical boundaries. If you want to find meaningful demographic data, your congregation needs to identify the geographical boundaries that interest you. For some congregations, this may be the entire community, a small town or neighborhood in which they are located. In other cases, a congregation may choose to look at their zip code and some specific surrounding zip codes. Since demographic data comes from the U.S. Census Bureau, this means a congregation may select specific census tracks that include and surround their facility.

A driving factor in defining the geographic area of interest is what your congregation wants to learn. Do you want to know characteristics of those close to your current location? Are you trying to identify the location of a particular group of persons that your congregation targets—Hispanics, young adults, gays and lesbians, immigrant populations, or some other group? In the former case, the geographical area you choose may be more limited to the area surrounding your place of worship—things like zip codes, census tracks, and radius from your current facility. In the latter, your geographical area may be much more extensive. Perhaps your congregation wants to serve Hispanics and, therefore, wants to use demographic data to discover where Hispanic populations are within the city. That means your area of interest might be an entire county or metropolitan area.

Available Information

The kinds of information available include, but are not limited to, ethnicity, income levels, educational levels, age distribution, home ownership, mobility, gender, employment, and household characteristics, such as married couple families, households with children, households with seniors, single-mom households, and single-dad households. Data about population decline or increase in a given area is also available. This information is gathered and distributed by the U.S. Census. American Factfinder is the Census Bureau's Web site for disseminating census data.[3] The data is free and relatively easy to access if you use the Internet. Some cities also post on their Web sites searchable demographic data largely or solely gleaned from census data. Some denominations do this too. Typically, these sites include only census data deemed most appropriate for congregational use, rather than all of the available census data.

Your congregation may have a member who does demographic research for his or her employer. If so, he or she could help your congregation retrieve appropriate information. But even if you need to do it yourself, it can be done. One congregation we worked with gathered two people from their sacred space team around a computer at the church. They then explored the demographic data posted on the city's Web site. Their small group approach was good. We have found that it is more effective to have one to three members of a sacred space team, rather than the entire team, investigate and present findings from the demographic data. Involving the entire team often complicates the process.

Another kind of demographic information is called *lifestyle data* or *psychographic data*. This data focuses on personality traits or behavior tendencies. A prominent distributor of this kind of data for congregations is Percept.[4] They have a sample of a demographic report provided to congregations on their Web site.

Percept draws data from several sources—the U.S. Census, Claritas, the WEFA Group, and the Ethos Survey Series. Claritas is a target marketing information company that offers demographic data, consumer behavior, marketing analysis services, and customer segmentation profiling that is often used by businesses to define their customer base. The WEFA Group provides forecasting data, especially economic analysis. The Ethos data source provides information from the largest survey of religious attitudes and behaviors of people living in the United States.

Percept has renamed Claritas's segmentation system "Lifestyles" and includes data that better reflects a church context. Examples of

Percept lifestyles include "Laboring Rural Families" or "Struggling Urban Life." Each of the fifty lifestyle segments is specifically described, including age ranges, economic and education levels, marital status, and housing, as well as faith involvement, contributions to congregations, primary concerns, and church program interests.

A helpful resource with specific instructions on how to maneuver in certain Web sites to obtain information about religious adherents, census data, and other community information is titled "Community Profile Builder" and is found on the Web site of the Association of Religion Data Archives.[5]

Observe Your Community

Demographics are not just gathered statistics about people in the congregation and community. They also include what you observe in your neighborhood and community. A congregation in a neighborhood where many people live below the poverty level noticed that its neighbors were taking cabs to the Laundromat because the closest Laundromat was too far away for people to walk with their laundry. The congregation purchased an old strip mall to turn it into assets for their community. The first space they renovated was for a neighborhood Laundromat, which they aptly called Flowing Waters.

Kevin Ford recommends visiting local supermarkets, retail shops, and fast-food restaurants with an eye to discovering what you can about the community. What can you tell about the ethnic makeup of the community by the kinds of food that are sold? What can you discover about the ages and family makeup of residents by the products that are prominently displayed? What do these places of business show you about the people in your community?[6]

We know a congregation that did this kind of "personal" demographics study by participating in their city's Study Circle program. Study circles are small community groups formed in neighborhoods in cities around the country that bring together groups of citizens to dialogue about issues such as race, neighborhoods, and families.[7] Members of this congregation also participated in their neighborhood association as an intentional effort to listen to the needs of the neighbors and to suggest how their congregation might help to serve those needs. This congregation is committed to discovering the needs of their neighbors.

Sometimes denominations pay a group membership to Percept that gives all of their congregations free access to Percept's demographic data. Other denominations aggregate census data for use by congregations. For example, the Church of the Nazarene Research Center maps Nazarene congregations in each state.[8] Those interested in information around an existing congregation or in an area targeted for a new church can define the radius from the church that they wish to explore. Data such as population growth rates, households with children, adult age groups, and so forth are then displayed in chart form. This data can be downloaded into an Excel spreadsheet.

Using such data sometimes means a congregation discovers a wide discrepancy between who they are, whom they imagine themselves serving, and the makeup of their neighboring community. This happened in an urban congregation that once served middle-class professionals who lived in their neighborhood. Over time, these professionals moved out of the neighborhood but continued commuting to their congregation. As the years passed, though, attendance dwindled because the congregation was no longer drawing professionals from the neighborhood. Instead, the congregation was located in the midst of a poverty-stricken area of the city. Circumstances such as these require much discussion and prayerful discernment to figure out what needs to take place. In this case, the membership decided to redefine their mission. They then bought a facility nearby and turned it into a community center to serve the poor in their neighborhood.

Another option for congregations that serve those who are not from their neighborhood is to relocate their place of worship closer to those they do serve. That's what a synagogue in Indianapolis did. They decided to relocate after facing the fact that the Jewish population of Indianapolis was no longer located near them but had, in fact, moved further north of the city.

Likewise, a Burmese congregation that began in a church north of the central part of the city because of connections with a friendly congregation soon realized that they needed to move to a location further south in the city where the Burmese immigrants tended to settle.

Finding out the characteristics of your congregation's neighbors is another way of answering the question, who are our neighbors? An urban congregation in Indianapolis takes a unique approach to learning about their neighbors. They do this through door-to-door visitation. Instead of focusing on their neighbors' needs, this congregation seeks to discover the gifts, skills, and interests of their neighbors. This way the congregation can affirm these people and give them places of service in the congregation. Their pastor tells how they discovered a neighborhood woman's passion for cooking and invited her to cook a meal for them. She soon was the "go to" person for cooking meals at the church. Her reputation as a great cook spread among members of the congregation. They began calling on her to serve food in other settings. This congregation discovered that evangelism is more than reaching out to serve others. It is also reaching out so that others can serve the church.

Trends and Assets

In addition to data about the people in a neighborhood and community, congregations also benefit from knowledge of the area's trends and assets. Trends are projected directions of population, economics, infrastructures, and other aspects of a community's future. Assets are the strengths and services that already exist in the community.[9] Both are important to congregations planning their mission and their facilities.

Exploration of trends includes questions, such as, is the overall population increasing or decreasing? Where are the pockets of growth? What is the economic health of the community? Are businesses and industries downsizing or hiring? Are new businesses being attracted to the area? If so, what kind?

A trend often overlooked by congregations is planned changes in infrastructure. These can be as simple as street widening affecting the available space on a congregation's campus or new highways that will make the congregation's property unusable. Infrastructure issues are some of the most difficult to deal with because infrastructures are planned far into the future and often change. A congregation in our sacred space program was told that their property would be bought and used to create an interchange for a major state highway. In light of that, the congregation bought thirteen acres across the street from their sanctuary. They built their education building on the new property in preparation for the state's buyout of the property where the sanctuary was located. Then another location was chosen for the interchange. The sanctuary property was not bought. The congregation found itself with an education building on one side of the street, a sanctuary on the other, and no funds from a buyout to build a new sanctuary near the education wing.

Other congregations, upon learning that within five to ten years a road extension would take their property, adopt a "wait and see" attitude. While that may sound wise, especially in light of the previous story, such an approach can catch a congregation off guard when they are notified that the work is about to begin. That happened to a congregation that contacted the Indianapolis Center for Congregations for assistance in finding another place of worship because they had limited time to vacate their building to allow for the highway in front of their building to be widened.

So how does a congregation discover the trends in its community? Your area planning commission is a good source for infrastructure and housing developments. You will also want to check community organizations, such as the United Way, economic development organizations, and school districts. They do periodic studies that offer a breadth of information about the services and needs of the community. Many communities have social services directories.

Another way of discovering trends in a community is for a congregation to invite a group of community leaders to discuss the trends they see in the community.[10] Realtors are another good source of information about trends and assets in a community.

In addition to trends, you will want to consider community assets. Assets are the strengths of an area. They include services such as day-care centers, senior citizen centers, community economic development organizations, banks, food pantries, Laundromats, grocery stores, transportation, churches, synagogues, schools, and much more.

Many congregations have visions of starting after-school programs, day-care centers, senior citizen centers, and other services. Such ministries can be meaningful expressions of a congregation's mission. But what if the community is already being sufficiently served by similar programs? Is it necessary for a congregation to start a senior center when another one thrives just three blocks away? Knowledge of community assets will help congregations avoid costly replication of existing services and other planning mistakes.

Considering how community assets, or lack of them, impact your proposed project is vital. A congregation that wanted to serve unwed mothers who needed health care planned to provide a clinic in their facility that would serve those needs. In their planning, they failed to consider that these mothers did not have cars and there were no bus routes to the congregation's facility.

Knowing the trends and assets of your community may seem to complicate your decision making. However, this knowledge, if seriously considered, can help your congregation shape your ministry to meet the actual needs of your neighbors.

Remember, understanding the characteristics of the population that surrounds your congregation will help shape your mission and, in turn, your facility. Are you called to offer a soup kitchen for the homeless nearby? Do senior citizens in your neighborhood need a place for study or recreation? Would young professionals find a full-service day-care center helpful? If your congregation decides to address these or other needs based on demographic information, such a decision will affect the kinds of changes you will want to make to your facility.

Congregational Demographics

In the same way you need information about your community, demographic data about your congregation is equally important. Do you know the age, marital status, and ethnicity of the members of your congregation now? How does that compare to the makeup of your neighborhood or community? Where do the members of your congregation live? Are there pockets of members in specific locations throughout your community? If so, what ministry(ies) might be started and/or moved to that location to serve not only your members in that area of the city, but also neighbors of those members? How many of your current members joined in the last five years? How many have been members more than twenty-five years? What is the makeup of those who have joined more recently compared to those who have attended twenty-five or more years? What is drawing your recent members to your congregation? Are there common characteristics among newer members that can be identified? The answers to these and other questions, perhaps unique to your congregation, can help shape your mission and define your needed facilities. What direction should you go with your three-floor building for a congregation that has many senior citizens? What facilities need to be examined and expanded if for the last three to five years your congregation has been attracting mostly young families?

There are several ways of finding the demographics of your congregation. In addition to its community data, Percept offers a congregational profile that enables users to compare the makeup of their congregation with the makeup of their community.

A low-cost way of discovering where your members live is using a map. Ask each household to put a pin marking where they live. You can use different colored pins to show the locations of more recent members in comparison to longtime members. Use of a map like this is only effective if there is a system of keeping track of which members have placed their pins on the map. When the map has a sufficient representation of the congregation, observations and implications can be discussed.

Your congregation could also choose to create its own survey. This can be done separately or be included in a survey the congregation takes about particular programming or congregational needs. Nancy Ammerman includes in her book *Congregation and Community* a congregational survey she used in studying congregations in changing communities.[11] You might want to use it to prompt your thinking about what questions you would like answered in your congregation. Ammerman's survey includes travel time from home to place of worship, length of membership, former denominational connections, number and ages of those in the household, level of education, years in the community, beliefs, ethnicity, and so on. Gil Rendle and Alice Mann's book *Holy Conversations: Strategic Planning as a Spiritual Practice for Congregations* also offers several suggestions for discovering more about your congregation's members.[12]

Sometimes congregations collect so much data that it seems overwhelming. How do you use it to help you discern God's call for your congregation? Rendle and Mann emphasize that data should be used to answer the questions you want answered.[13] For example, perhaps your question is, what is the ethnic and economic makeup of the population living within a five-mile radius of our church? Or you might ask, what are the ages of people who have joined our congregation in the last five years? You can use this information to discuss its effect on your facilities. Depending on the questions of interest to you, your congregation may rethink the questions you ask new members. That way demographic information about your congregation can be included in church management software or traditional files and accessed for future reference.

An honest look at demographics, both external to the congregation and internal, means that a congregation has to be willing to change. There is no sense investing the time collecting and analyzing demographic data if the congregation as a whole is happy with the status quo. That said, congregations that take the time to learn about their neighbors can more effectively reaffirm their mission and develop their facilities to achieve it.

Summary for the Team

- One aspect of the discern phase of the sacred space model is asking, "Who are our neighbors?" Congregations can discover answers to that question by investigating demographics.
- Useful demographic data requires an intentional identification of the geographic area of interest to the congregation.
- Demographic data of interest to congregations includes data about people who live in the congregation's geographic area of interest, information about your community's trends and assets, and data about current members of your congregation.
- Rather than starting with data, congregations need to start by articulating the question(s) they seek to answer and then pursuing the data that will help them answer that question.
- Demographic data serves as a discussion starter that can lead a congregation to refine or reaffirm its mission and evaluate its space in relation to that mission.

Questions for the Team

1. How does your congregation learn about your neighbors?
2. If you have not already done so, how might you determine the geographic area of interest to your congregation? Who needs to be involved in that discussion and decision making?
3. What questions does your congregation have that could be answered by demographic information? What kinds of data would you need to provide the answers?
4. Once you have gathered information, who will discuss its implications? How and when?
5. What effect on your facilities can you envision knowledge of demographics making for your congregation?

CHAPTER 3 Who Is God Calling
Us to Be?

Mission

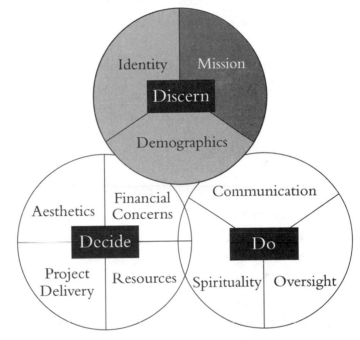

$\mathcal{A}$ nursery worker nestles a baby in her arms. At her feet sit
three toddlers playing with puppets. A helper gets two other children bowls of Cheerios. A kindergartner hums "Amazing Grace" as
he drifts through the room. Things have not always been this way.
A few months ago, the nursery at this church was almost empty.
This congregation was divided, not by conflict, but by a busy street
separating the sanctuary from the education building.

Their new nursery didn't appear magically. Thought and prayer
went into deciding what to do about two buildings separated by

cars rushing by. There were many options. The congregation could keep things the way they were. After all, change comes at a price, and some things are best left alone. They considered tearing down the old sanctuary and building a new one on the same side as the education building. They also considered moving the sanctuary by having large trucks and various other kinds of machinery lift it and move it across the road and place it next to the education wing. There were other options as well. But before they could discern what was best, they had to answer one question: who is God calling us to be?

Values, Mission, and Vision

A major phase in any building project's *discern* period is naming what God is calling your congregation to be. This is a three-step process to clarify values, mission, and vision. By values, we mean the principles the congregation regards as most important. Mission expresses the congregation's primary purpose. Vision pictures the congregation's future as the mission comes to life.

Oftentimes congregations treat building issues as if they are all about routine maintenance concerns, such as taking out the trash. Some are routine. However, the way a congregation handles even routine maintenance tasks needs to be part of a larger plan that considers values, mission, and vision.

Some people stay away from dealing with building issues in terms of strategic questions because such issues stir emotions and may lead to conflicts. This is why issues related to your congregation's facility have to be handled with care and why it is important to step back and look at the total strategic direction your congregation is heading.

Most building issues—beyond taking out the trash—are complex. Whether you improve the lighting in the sanctuary or build a new facility across town, discernment about your values, mission, and vision leads to better decisions and results in outcomes more consistent with your congregation's positive identity.

The account of the building of the Tower of Babel is a good example of a faith community so sure of its project that it moved ahead without thinking strategically—which includes thinking theologically. Their purpose was to build a tower that would reach to the heavens so that they might make a name for themselves and not be scattered over the face of the earth. The Lord, however, was displeased with their plan and did just the thing they had hoped to avoid—he scattered them by confusing their language so they couldn't understand one another. Endeavors entered into without discernment and God's direction are doomed.

So how do you begin considering your congregation's values, mission, and vision as part of a building process? First, more than just the sacred space team needs to be invested. The governing board and people from the congregation need to be part of the conversation. Many congregations already communicate common values and a shared sense of mission and vision, so not every sacred space team has to start from scratch. Whether you are starting from square one or reviewing your current process, you want to set aside two to three meetings to look over, talk about, and come to a deeper understanding of your stated congregational personality. You will find it helpful to invite people who were part of the process of identifying these principles to be part of your conversation. It is critical to do this for all building projects, even small ones. Teams that spend time in the discern phase thinking about what God calls them to be are always more satisfied with their work on their building.

Moving Deliberately

Moving ahead without reflecting on congregational values can create problems. That's what happened when members of a rural church noticed their toilets didn't flush right. Building issues often involve such practical concerns! The building committee walked around the outside of the sanctuary and noticed a large maple tree growing right at the fence separating the church property from a thick, green cornfield. "That's it," one of them said; "those roots are ruining our septic system." After worship the next week, the building committee met to address the tree problem and decided to cut down the tree. After a crew cut the tree, the men divided the spoils, taking firewood for the fall.

The next week the pastor received a letter from the man who owned the cornfield. The farmer's tone was polite, but he suggested that the church check the Ten Commandments the next time they thought of cutting down one of his trees. He wrote, "If you had checked with me, it wouldn't have been stealing. I would have said 'yes.' However, you didn't. What kind of example does that set for the children?"

The congregation went against one of their values, obvious, if unstated, about relationships just so they could move their building issue along. In the end, they discovered it wasn't a problem with roots at all. The soft maple had a shallow root structure. All they needed was a good plumber.

Some of us like fixing problems quickly. Resist this tendency when it comes to building issues. Remember, building issues relate to larger, strategic questions. Certainly, there are times when problems need to be addressed promptly—rain drips from the roof onto the organ or the pastor notices a gas leak. What sacred space teams need to do with nonemergency building issues is take a breath, engage their brains collectively, and practice faith disciplines. This is not to slow the process down, but rather to get it moving at the right speed.

The best way to set the appropriate pace is to address building issues from a strategic perspective. If your congregation does not have clear statements about values, mission, and vision, the sacred space team needs to work with others from the congregation to create a shared understanding of these principles. This may slow down the process. Yet moving slowly at this stage allows the team to move effectively later. This is an example of the positive nature of delayed gratification: it is strategic rather than reactive.

As we said earlier in this chapter, to create clear statements about your congregation's identity, you will want members of your sacred space team to be part of a larger process or invite others to join the process. Different congregations will do this differently. Some sacred space teams enter a building project with a clear idea of their values, mission, and vision. Other teams will review such ideas and find that they are no longer accurate. They will want to go back to the governing board and/or dig deeper. Some teams will find that their congregation has no applicable statements about values, mission, and vision. Such teams will want to encourage their governing council to pray and think clearly about congregational identity and work on articulating it clearly. The process described below is adaptable to almost any situation.

The Importance of Values

Start with *values*. Values are thoughts and behaviors that people regard as most important. Values express your congregation's standards of ideas and actions. These values should convey your highest aspirations.

Naming values is not an exercise that should bend to lowest common denominators. You are looking to identify core aspects of your congregation. They are best expressed positively. Values are often nouns, such as "acceptance" or "zeal." A list of values may include adventure, awe, freedom, holiness, humility, joy, peace, and the three noted by the apostle Paul—faith, hope, and love. Of course, these are merely illustrative. You'll want to develop your own list.

The sacred space team's challenge is not coming up with values. There are many. The challenge is to understand your congregation's *shared* values. One way to do that is by naming a positive event and then describing it. Ask the group to identify the values that supported the event. One congregation doing this exercise used the example of their annual Apple Festival. Almost the entire congregation participated. What made it so much fun? Team members identified values of unity and joy. This told the sacred space team that not only should their building express a common spirit and a sense of delight, but their process should too.

An exercise like this also helped a Roman Catholic congregation in Indianapolis. In worship, people sit in the round. The congregation believes that it is important for people to see faces and not backs. Relationships matter. When you walk into worship, the first thing you see is an image of their patron saint. Her eyes look upward, suggesting a focus on God.

However, when this parish's sacred space team met for the first time, it was hard for them to focus. It wasn't from lack of ideas. The problem was that people had too many specific ideas: build a new building, renovate, add on, keep things the same. So the team made a smart move. They put the brakes on their preconceived notions and went into a period of discernment. They began by having members tell the story of how they came to this parish. They described first impressions and why they stayed. They found they shared common values even if they did have different ideas. Their common values included their Catholic faith and their desire for hospitality and authenticity.

The group discovered that their building didn't need replacing. Their dozens of ideas narrowed to three or four manageable and helpful ones. They discerned it was time to improve and enhance existing parts of the building so their building would be an instrument of faith and a home for hospitality. Their direction matched their values.

In their book *Cracking Your Congregation's Code*, Richard Southern and Robert Norton suggest a three-step process to identify key values. First, you identify three to five essential values. Second, you define them in writing. Say precisely what each of these values means. The third step is to prioritize them.[1] Their book has a "Core Values Survey" to help you identify and prioritize your most vital attributes.[2]

A way of checking if the values you have identified are true for your congregation is to show a photo of the most beloved place in your facility. Then ask, "What values do you see?" Match the responses against the values previously named. Do they connect? If not, where are the differences between what the building says and what the people say they value?

Your Congregation's Unique Mission

Once you have a good sense of your congregation's core values, you can work toward a *mission statement*. As noted earlier, if you already have a mission statement that does not need revision, use this time to learn how it was developed and what it means now to the congregation. If you need to develop a mission statement, make sure that you have the right people from your congregation involved. Who the right people are for your congregation depends partly on your culture and polity. Besides that, though, the qualities that make a person the right person include having a passion for the future of the congregation, being able to work well with others, having an ability to understand complex issues, and possessing the willingness to give the necessary time to the project. Consult with your clergy leader and your governing board. Working on this kind of discernment affects the whole congregation.

Your mission statement needs to be shaped by your core values. According to Gil Rendle and Alice Mann in *Holy Conversations*, useful mission statements identify what you believe, where you serve, your target audience, and what gifts support your unique mission.[3] Southern and Norton say that a mission statement should describe your congregation, what your view of transformation is, and how you intend to carry out this mission.[4] As you review your statement (or help create one), be aware that this is going to be a work in progress. Mission statements need to be updated frequently. They are never the final word. Your goal is to understand your mission well enough so that whatever you do to your building will support your mission.

Surveys are helpful in this process. In chapter 2 we introduced you to ways in which demographic surveys help you identify the characteristics of your congregants. This information can help you clarify your mission. Another form of congregational survey is the internal assessment survey. Internal assessments are surveys that help you identify what your members and other constituents appreciate most. Such internal assessments help you identify strengths that reflect your highest values. Surveys that you create can help start the thinking process. However, such surveys exist in a data vacuum. The best surveys are those with data, not just opinion, behind them. Without that data, you don't have any information for comparison.

Two surveys that have thorough data sets behind them are the Transforming Church Index and the U.S. Congregational Life Survey. The Transforming Church Index (produced by TAG) is an online instrument designed to identify organizational assets and opportunities for improvement.[5] This instrument measures key factors often overlooked, including the ability of leaders to define healthy role boundaries and the congregation's ability to embrace change.

The U.S. Congregational Life Survey measures ten strengths. Among these are growing spiritually, caring for children and youth, and welcoming new people. It works very simply. First, your constituents take the survey. Then you compare your results to other congregations' results. For example, the degree to which you welcome new people will be compared to how other congregations do the same. By comparing your information to that which has been gathered from thousands of others, you have a more accurate view of your strengths and weaknesses. Such appraisals are not based on subjective judgment. By interpreting the data in relationship to other data sets, the process becomes objective. Ultimately, you can use this information to create or recreate your mission statement that in turn informs decisions you make about your facility. The U.S. Congregational Life Survey is easy to complete (you have worshipers fill it out during a service).[6]

These tools won't magically provide you with a mission statement, but they will help you objectively identify your congregation's strengths. And awareness of your strengths will help you write a mission statement.

Kevin Ford suggests that a congregation answer three questions as way to begin to develop a mission statement.[7]

1. What is our congregation most passionate about?
2. What do we have the capacity to be the best at (compared with other congregations)?
3. What is our overarching reason for existence?

Once these questions are discussed thoroughly and answered in several congregational contexts, your leaders can develop a mission statement incorporating the responses.

A mission statement should not only reflect your congregation's special strengths, but also tell others what makes your faith community unique. In doing so, it will effectively guide your building program. A mission statement declares your positive core identity and purpose in succinct terms. Here is an example of a mission statement:

> The First Community Congregation believes God calls us to be the light of love to all those we meet. We are a people who worship God by offering care to all those we encounter, in our town and across the world.

The process of discernment helps a congregation develop a mission statement.

Connecting Your Mission to Your Building

Once a mission statement is complete, it can serve as a focus for further reflection about all aspects of congregational life, including building projects. That is what happened when one Lutheran congregation used the season of Lent as a time of discernment. Their primary tool was their mission statement, which says, "Our mission is to live as God's servants in the world as we proclaim, reflect, and celebrate the love and grace of Jesus Christ." They met in small groups and talked about their mission statement. What did each phrase mean? Sitting face-to-face, they talked about how their congregational programs and services helped them serve God in this world. They also talked about how their mission was connected to potential changes to the building. Sometimes the questions were challenging. Should we move? Do we have enough money? Can our building help us celebrate Christ's love and grace? As one member observed, "This was an intense Lent." But it was probably a good Lent. That's because, as Kevin Ford says, if your mission statement has never forced you to answer a tough question or make an unpopular decision, then it's probably not effective.

Through the process, it became clear that the mission would shape the building plans, not the other way around. This Lutheran congregation concluded their process with a celebration dinner. They took reservations. Then more people showed up than had made reservations. The organizers scrambled to set up extra tables and chairs. Servers eyed the casseroles nervously as people continued to arrive. The leader of the sacred space team said, "There's nothing like talking about starting a building program and then running out of space for the big dinner."

In this case, the sacred space team did not have to jump-start the process of creating a new mission statement. It made good use of the existing mission statement. Participants were willing to stop, think, and pray before they started deciding. By doing so, the project, whatever they decided, would be more in line with their mission than if they had started with architectural drawings of a proposed building.

Later, when the congregation was well into the project, the congregation's sacred space leader was asked to name the most helpful part of the process. "Of all the things we did," she said, "the most helpful was when we discussed elements of our mission statement to better understand what we needed to do."

Creating a Vision Statement

All of the earlier discernment processes take you to the place where you are ready to create a vision statement. Recall that you begin with your values, that which you hold as most important. Then you expand on your values by creating a mission statement, a succinct declaration of who you are as a congregation. You then build upon your values and your stated mission to develop a vision statement. As Rendle and Mann note, "A vision statement is a word picture of what our congregation would look like if we were, in fact, able to fulfill our mission statement."[8] Vision statements help people imagine a positive future. A well-designed vision statement is easy to understand, inspires the congregation, reinforces the stated values, develops the mission statement more fully, and uses present tense, active verbs and nouns that paint a picture. Below is an example of a congregational vision statement:

> The First Community congregation swings open its door to all who seek to love God and neighbor more deeply. With energy and excellence, we grow in love for the sake of God's kingdom. Our sanctuary overflows with affection for this good life.

Think of values as the foundation that supports mission and vision. See your mission statement as an expression of the positive present. Understand vision statements as the developing future reality.

Discernment Is Essential

A process of discernment can inform every building project. Sometimes building projects go awry because of conflict. Sometimes they run into trouble because sacred space teams choose the wrong vendors or a congregation runs out of money. Such problems can likely be traced to inadequate discernment. Discernment is essential because there is a kind of "pay me now or pay me later" dynamic involved in planning.

For people who want to move a project along, the time it takes for discernment will be frustrating. But it will likewise be frustrating for those who like to ponder a long while, because healthy discernment has its own forward momentum. It moves incrementally and in stages but is not snagged on minutiae. It is thoughtful but does not lag. Moving too slowly is like pouring a bucket of water on the early flash of flame of a bonfire. Moving too fast is like pouring gasoline on a fire—you get a dangerous flash that burns away clear thinking.

In this and the previous chapters, we have taken you through steps in the discern phase of our sacred space model. As you leave the discern phase, it is important to be intentional about your team's move to the decide phase, all the while realizing that there will be points along the way when you will want to step back and prayerfully discern where you are headed. As you move toward the decide phase, you may find some transitional exercises helpful. For example, now may be a good time to brainstorm the decision points that lie ahead for your project, make a thorough report to the congregation, or assign team members to search out the best resources.

A Discernment Exercise

One helpful exercise is called the "pre-mortem."[9] At the end of naming and/or evaluating the congregation's values, mission statement, and vision statement, the team responds to this question: "Suppose that three years from now this building project has failed. What is it that has gone wrong?" Individuals are given a moment to write down their answers and then are invited to share them with the team.

One person may say, "We moved too fast." Another may answer, "We didn't check in with the whole congregation enough." Yet another says, "We didn't make sure the architect listened to us."

Using the pre-mortem tool enables the observations of individuals to shed light on the group's blind spots. In addition to naming potential challenges in the building project, using the pre-mortem also provides a glimpse of the expertise of those in the group. The assumption is that what one identifies as a possible glitch is an area he or she knows something about. The more things that are identified, the more expertise is held by individuals in the group. It is good to get this expertise out on the table. Being able to articulate only three or four things that might have gone wrong indicates that a group is not particularly invested in the process or that they don't have a lot of experience with it. Naming many possible glitches is a sign that a group is not only highly engaged but also has expertise to address the challenges ahead.

Another benefit of the pre-mortem exercise is that it provides the team a way to expose defense mechanisms and breaks the silence related to difficult topics. Furthermore, it helps lay the foundation for handling conflict constructively. When dealing with buildings, we address one of the most emotionally laden aspects of congregational life. All kinds of variables make the emotional response more or less powerful depending on the circumstance. Many beautiful sanctuaries stir powerful feelings simply because of their beauty. People are also emotionally attached to congregation buildings because they represent, at some level, home. They are God's shelters. A man sits in the same pew he sat in at his father's memorial service. A young woman stands in the back of a sanctuary and beholds the altar of her first communion. Things like that stir strong feelings. They should.

The Academy of Neuroscience for Architecture (ANFA) studies the emotional responses people have to sacred space. They haven't figured out the exact dynamics, but they have measured a variety of emotional responses that demonstrate that buildings for worship ignite human chemistry. Spaces stir a whole range of emotional responses: awe, mystery, anxiety, comfort, and much more. Some buildings bring strong emotional responses because the people contemplating change are the same ones who built the structure in the first place. Their emotional response is similar to moving from a home and watching the new occupants chop down the oak tree you watched your kids climb. Also, people may feel like they have ownership of the building. When a change is made, even a change as subtle as moving the painting of the Last Supper from the narthex to the pastor's study, it can be a touchy subject. We all know that there are times spouses disagree on how to change or adapt a home. Just multiply this dynamic by how many members feel ownership over the building, and you can watch the emotional resistance to change rise with the number of opinions expressed.

A pre-mortem gets these defense mechanisms out in the open. By sharing negative scenarios, the group, paradoxically, is more likely to recognize beginnings of conflict and make early course corrections. The possibility of self-deception is not erased but is minimized. If someone has a nagging, unexpressed sense that the architect isn't listening, a member of the group is more likely to say this aloud because it has already been named in the pre-mortem. Problems or apprehensions are normalized rather than ignored. Self-deception is replaced with truth telling.

The primary rule of discernment is to think before you act. Since many people do not think of the mind as directly connected to the soul or the heart, they often downplay how important careful thinking is to congregational life. But when dealing with the complexity of building improvements, one of the best God-given assets is a clear and thoughtful mind.

We know that building issues are complex. Think about a home building project you know. Was it a seamless, smooth process, with no problems whatsoever? And if you were building it with a friend or a spouse or a sibling, did you agree on every detail? It should come as no surprise that a congregation is going to find it challenging to move smoothly through a building process. However, the discern, decide, and do model makes the building process—large or small—more manageable with much more positive results. When a congregation learns to address building issues well, all kinds of potential is unleashed. A new set of programs, and sometimes a new way of life together, is established. Once you learn to tackle building issues well, hardly any issue will bowl you over. You will be ready to handle any number of congregational issues extremely well.

Yes, discernment is the first act. Do it well and you will be ready to move toward decisions.

Summary for the Team

- Discerning your mission is a three-phase process that involves clarifying values, mission, and vision.
- Values are the principles the congregation regards most important. Mission expresses the congregation's primary purpose. Vision imagines the congregation's future as the mission comes to life.
- Almost all building projects should connect to larger, strategic congregational issues.
- Mission should shape the building plans, not the other way around.
- When a congregation learns to address building issues well, all kinds of potential is activated. Once you learn to tackle building issues well, hardly any issue will bowl you over.

Questions for the Team

1. What is the mission of your congregation?
2. How would you characterize the values that support your mission?
3. What are the differences between what the building says and what members of your congregation say they value?
4. How will your building project help your congregation be measurably different five years from now?
5. What is your congregation most passionate about, and how does this connect with plans to enhance your facility?

PART 2
DECIDE

CHAPTER 4 What Do We Want Our
Building to Convey?

Aesthetics

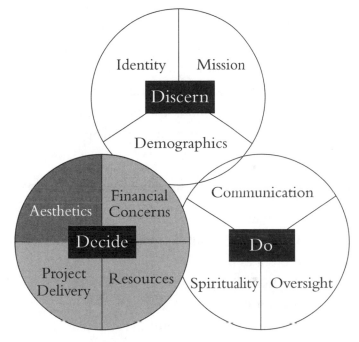

W hat does a congregational building look like? In the past,
they were fairly uniform and recognizable, adorned with peaked
roofs, steeples, crosses, stone Torahs. Today, however, there are all
kinds of congregational buildings. Some are dignified cathedral-style
edifices. Some are storefronts or pole buildings. Some have grounds
landscaped like an estate. Others don't have many trees or shrubs but
have large parking lots with good signage. Some buildings have office
spaces fancier than some Fortune 500 offices. Others have offices so
packed that you see stacks of paper everywhere.

Not only do congregational buildings look different, but they communicate many different messages about many different ideas. Martin and Micah Marty's book *Our Hope for Years to Come* contains written reflections and photographs of places of worship.[1] The point of the book, according to the Martys, was to capture the *idea* represented by each of these places. The photographs, all in black and white, are crisp, clear, and beautiful. Open the book and you see arches seeking the sky and pews rooted in marble. Most of the photos show Gothic gathering spaces, though Micah Marty also took pictures of modest wood-frame churches on the Great Plains.

The Martys' book captures architectural work implying traditional aspects of sanctuary. David Spero's *Churches* and Camilo José Vergara's *How the Other Half Worships* show congregations expressing other ideas.[2] Focusing on evangelical charismatic and inner-city African American and Latino congregations, these books present congregational buildings completely different from those in the Martys' book. And the messages these buildings communicate are different as well.

One of the strengths of such books is that they help us think about how and what congregational buildings communicate. The Martys' book is especially helpful because it is divided thematically. Each section describes an idea, and a photograph of a building represents the idea. Some of the ideas illustrated by the photographs are shelter, love, awe, silence, depth, brightness, joy, glory, generosity, access, and revelation.

Qualities Your Building Conveys

Think about your building. What parts of your building communicate the above qualities? Are there other qualities that your building conveys?

As we said earlier, buildings communicate. One way to think about what buildings communicate is to address aesthetics. "Aesthetics" refers to elements of the building that convey positive qualities pleasing to the senses. In short, aesthetics is about beauty.

Aesthetic issues are part of the *decide* phase of the discern, decide, and do model. They raise questions such as these: What do we want our building to convey? How do we want our building to look? What do we want people to feel or to think about when they are in this space? Asking good questions about what your building says helps you consider your building's aesthetics.

Your building should be beautiful. Chances are you have seen and appreciated a magnificent, elaborate cathedral. Likewise, you may have walked into a simple meetinghouse and thought, "This is awesome." By saying your building should be beautiful, we are not advocating one design over another. We are saying that buildings communicate a clear, specific message connected to congregational identity, and that message should be communicated beautifully.

That's because a beautiful building encourages beautiful thoughts and behavior. Theologian Edward Farley says that beauty supports virtue. In this sense, beauty is not the same as nice looks or good taste.[3] Instead, beauty is that which inspires us to live fully human, or, as the book of Galatians names, by exhibiting the fruit (virtues) of the Spirit: love, joy, peace, patience, kindness, generosity, faithfulness, gentleness, and self-control (Galatians 5:22-23). You want your facility to express outwardly the virtues most important to your mission.

During the decide phase of your project, you will work with those on your team as well as with others, such as architects or designers, to figure out how best to create space that serves a purpose and is pleasing. Many questions related to aesthetics are best worked on with a professional. Nevertheless, you do not have to be an architect or a trained designer to think carefully about aesthetics. Taking time to think about design can help you to form wise questions about aesthetics to ask design professionals and those on your sacred space team.

When you do so, you'll find your team addressing a basic human need. Humans seek beauty. We don't seek ugliness. We are born with hearts that long for that which is aesthetically pleasing. The lyrics of a folk song by Jim Croegaert capture our desire for splendor:

Frost on the window

Is never the same

So many patterns

Fit in the frame

Captured in motion

Frozen in flame

Is there a Name

Why do we hunger for beauty?[4]

God calls us to create beauty. So what constitutes beauty? Frank Burch Brown, professor of Religion and the Arts at Christian Theological Seminary in Indianapolis, writes, "The reasons why an aesthetic work or style is good or bad, weak or strong (and in what circumstances), can never be expressed fully in words; yet they can often be pointed out through comparative and repeated looking and listening."[5]

Think in terms of your five senses. What makes a space pleasing to touch? To look at? How should sound play in the space you are designing? What should the space smell like? Color, smell, sound, touch, and even taste work together to create a room that is pleasing—or irritating. Perhaps that is why Psalm 27:4 connects God's beauty with God's presence in the temple:

One thing I asked of the LORD,
    that will I seek after:
to live in the house of the LORD
    all the days of my life,
to behold the beauty of the LORD,
    and to inquire in his temple.

Our religious buildings should not leave us hungry for beauty.

Design Matters

Discussions about aesthetics are tricky. It is hard to talk about aesthetics without sharing one's likes and dislikes. One person's idea of proportion may not be another's. Two elders look at the same pulpit. One says, "Beautiful, just beautiful." The other says, "It looks like the preacher is rising out of a tank." The difference arises because what is pleasing to one person is not necessarily pleasing to another. That's why so much has been written about the pros and cons of different designs for religious communities. The book *Ugly as Sin* by Michael Rose is a grumpy rant against Roman Catholic gathering spaces that are influenced, in his opinion, far too much by secular forces.[6] There is disagreement among building professionals, as well as congregational leaders, about whether traditional schools of architecture or more functional design/build methods should be used for sacred spaces. Which is more important—traditional values or functionality? How do you decide between liturgical and/or other guidelines for space and more entrepreneurial ideas geared toward bringing seekers into the building?

Many kinds of buildings are appropriate for congregations. Some introduce you to God who is fundamentally transcendent, farther from you than earth is from the sun. Some introduce you to God who is closer to you than you are to yourself. Some buildings are filled with sacred images, and in others the decorations are limited to one-hundred-year-old clear windows. Some buildings are containers for sacraments. Some are copies of business suites or shopping malls so that one feels "at ease" with God.

Your sacred space team will want to address such differences before it chooses a design aesthetic. Since people often feel strongly about matters of taste, your team will want to arrive at some general aesthetic guidelines before engaging an architect or designer. That way all involved will understand one another, even if they aren't on the same page, when it is time to create designs.

Frank Burch Brown again provides some helpful advice. Regarding matters of taste, he writes, "It is an act of Christian love to learn to appreciate or at least respect what others value in a particular style or work that they cherish in worship or in the rest of life. That is different, however, from personally liking every form of commendable art, which is impossible and unnecessary."[7]

What makes consideration of aesthetics so very important? The aesthetics of a building shape human beliefs and behavior. Gretchen Buggein describes this in a review of books on church architecture. Buggein provides a survey of literature about what contemporary congregational buildings communicate in both good and bad ways. She synthesizes it this way:

> Some verticality, a feeling of tradition and permanence, and at least a degree of formality do seem characteristics of most effective church spaces. These characteristics require both good design and its effective realization through high-quality materials and workmanship.
>
> Yet somewhere in the building process, issues of design need to be considered, because design does matter. Human beings have long

recognized that architecture shapes behavior and experience. We live in a material world and respond to what we see and feel, often quite unconsciously. Thoughtful church architects ask congregations what they want the church to do spiritually as well as functionally.[8]

What does your sacred space team want to communicate spiritually as well as functionally?

Associations and Connections

As you consider what you want your facility to communicate, think about how aesthetics relates to associations and connections. The stronger the association and connection between people and the new or renovated space, the more likely the space will reinforce positive behaviors and beliefs. Sacred spaces communicate powerfully when a community experiences connections between what it values the most and what constitutes the space.

For example, a congregant may sit in a pew made by her grandfather. Or a new building stands on a parcel of property given by one of the "saints" of the congregation. These relational connections are stronger than simply good design. They add to the attributes of good design.

Over time these connections get stronger. They develop. That is, two generations ago a family may have funded stained glass for the sanctuary. Now the congregation is moving the sanctuary. What happens to the stained-glass window? This question is more than a technical one. It is an aesthetic question. It is an aesthetic question because people must consider whether the windows fit the design of the new space. Will they look beautiful? However, the question of the stained-glass window is an aesthetic question in a broader sense as well. After all, there is such a thing as an aesthetic of relationships. Likewise, there is an aesthetic of faith and even of the use of artifacts in new settings. A congregation needs to negotiate questions raised by issues of connections and memory. Those responsible for an older building will want to understand and respect sacred memories. Those designing a new building will want to incorporate memory as well as expect and welcome new connections.

So, remember that aesthetics is about more than taste. It is about how beauty supports virtue. The aesthetics of a building communicates what you believe. And as we just observed, aesthetics involves keeping memory alive and making connections.

The Barn

These issues were considered in different ways by three congregations in our sacred space program that had very different design challenges. For Northview Christian Life Center, the challenge involved a 120-year-old barn, a structure once part of a Purdue University experimental farm. The task was how to transform the barn so that it supported the virtue of hospitality. For the St. Joan of Arc Catholic congregation, the challenge was to learn more about Roman basilica design before making decisions regarding renovation. Their task was to communicate belief. And Zion United Church of Christ needed to think about ways to improve two buildings separated by a busy city street. Their task involved keeping memory alive. As you read these cases, see if you can identify ways in which issues of taste, matters of beliefs and behaviors, and the importance of memory and connection were addressed.

When you look out where Northview Christian Life Center is located, you see a 13,000-square-foot high-tech building. You also see a barn more than a century old owned by the congregation since

1985. Recently the leaders of the church figured it was time to decide whether to keep the barn. The 1880 structure did not exactly fit the contemporary design of the rest of the campus, yet it communicated a quiet charm, a casual sense of God's goodness. Like a watercolor painting of a red barn hanging in a neighbor's family room, the old barn appears friendly, though from another time. The rest of Northview's facility is contemporary. Though it looks very different from the barn, it has been designed to be welcoming. The leaders wondered if there was a way to make good use of the obsolete barn rather than tear it down. After all, Northview's campus, though not rural, is surrounded by acres of green fields.

The congregation agreed on a project to renovate the barn so that it would be a welcoming place. Sociologist Ray Oldenburg writes about the importance of "the great, good place."[9] He calls it "celebrating the third place," the place that provides tranquility, informality, and friendliness. In society, such places are the small-town diner, independent bookstores, and artist cooperatives. Such "great, good places" are not the same as branded stores that create an aura of familiarity (and even intimacy) through branding, not reality. Chain restaurants that promote themselves as the neighborhood gathering places, while located in strip malls, are false attempts at being "great, good places." The barn, however, is an example of the "real thing."

The sacred space project director notes that now—after its renovation—there are plenty of windows in the barn. It looks out on eighty acres of beautiful rolling hills. You walk in and see an area that is wide open yet invites people to small group conversations. There is family room space on one side and a bar for side-by-side chats on the other. "People who are not churched and maybe even turned off by the church or have had bad experiences somewhere along the line come in, and right away a lot of those barriers come down," their project director says. "It's a very friendly, safe, relaxed place to be."

The barn at Northview Christian Life is designed to be a gathering place for people to meet beyond the home or workplace. It has a social aesthetic. Its fundamental meaning is to communicate social interaction with God and neighbor. Inside the barn, people feel at ease. Conversation flows.

If your sacred space team wants to design a friendly, good place to gather, they need to consider a variety of aesthetic questions. How do you design a place that doesn't get too loud when large numbers of people start talking? Is there room for comfortable seating so that people can linger? What colors suggest warm relationships?

If you are designing a gathering place for small groups, you need to consider the following aesthetic values: empathy, care, company, depth, sharing, comfort, and reassurance. What do members of your sacred space team associate with these words? What buildings or rooms communicate this to them in arenas of life outside congregational life?

Some designers suggest that wide-open spaces are less conducive to conversation than smaller, cozier rooms. Others feel that wide-open gathering spaces create a sense of being part of a larger group adventure. These are the sorts of values you will want to make decisions about if you are working on relational or gathering space for your congregation.

A Contemporary Basilica

For the Northview Christian Life Center, an old barn on their property provided them an opportunity to create a gathering space that communicated hospitality. St. Joan of Arc Catholic Church faced a very different circumstance. Their opportunity was in the form of their sanctuary, a towering structure in the style of a Roman basilica.

If you stood in the center of any major Roman city during the second century, chances are you could look up and see a basilica. People entered the basilicas to conduct business, pay their bills, purchase household items, and make travel reservations. After Constantine declared Christianity the state religion in the fourth century, Christians built sanctuaries in the basilica style. They co-opted the secular design of the basilica for their own purposes. Construction on St. Peter's, in Rome, may have been begun as early as 319 CE. This large sanctuary, holding more than three thousand people, is shaped like a long rectangle, though both ends are rounded. Worshipers process down a long center aisle, headed toward the altar at the eastern end.

The stately basilicas signified Christianity moving from a small band of folks operating at the edge of society to a faith celebrated and supported by those in power. The simplicity and rawness of the house church was being replaced by the complexity and grandeur of the basilica. Faith was becoming more public, and architectural aesthetics reflected this.

While St. Joan of Arc, located on the north side of Indianapolis, is far from fourth-century Rome, its large sanctuary is in the Roman basilica style. Completed in 1929, this Indianapolis sanctuary is almost an exact replica of Rome's St. Paul Outside the Walls. Not long ago, its exterior needed to be cleaned and the bell tower repaired. Inside, the floor tile was peeling apart. That's because, when the building was originally constructed, the congregation ran out of funds and chose not to put down sturdy terrazzo flooring.

St. Joan of Arc's sacred space team didn't want a renovation to ruin the essence of the Roman basilica. Remember, buildings shape thoughts and behavior. Significant change to the basilica could result in unwanted change in the congregation's relationship with God.

To help them learn what was essential to the design, they invited a local priest to talk about the meaning of the basilica. "You can't help but notice the tall ceilings," he told them. "You can't help but be guided there by the light coming from the windows. The entire structure is designed to make you want to look up."

So look up they did. Now members not only appreciate the beauty of their worship space, but also experience the awe-inspiring feeling of looking outside and beyond themselves. As this congregation continues to renovate its sacred space, it keeps in mind the aesthetics of the Roman basilica. They won't make the space into something it's not. The sanctuary communicates God's transcendence. You enter the building and sense deep down that you are part of something larger and more beautiful than your own life. This is the virtue of gratitude at work. It's a value worth maintaining.

The Education Building

Basilicas aren't part of the usual Midwest aesthetic. An entirely different situation from Joan of Arc's challenged members of the Zion United Church of Christ as they walked into their education wing. They felt that an institutional style building that looked more like a 1960s school than a church negatively influenced the first impression their church gave. Their education building stood in contrast to their beautiful, older sanctuary located across the city street. As they looked at their education wing, they saw more than a youth room needing new paint; they saw the need to improve what the whole facility communicated. As one leader said, "Everybody who drives by our education building thinks it is a school. People don't make the connection that it goes with our sanctuary, which is across the street."

The congregation wanted to do more than strengthen the association between the sanctuary and the education wing. They also didn't want to lose good memories of and strong connections with those who had come before them. To help them get a handle on what they needed, they visited four churches that had recently completed renovations. They were amazed at what they saw and learned. When they walked into one church, a simple block building, it was so bright and shiny that everyone assumed it was new. They soon learned that this particular facility was built the same year as theirs—1962. This experience taught them that they did not need a sparkling new building. Taking care of and updating their present facility could produce a home for their congregation that was aesthetically pleasing.

Based on their visits to these other churches, the members of the Zion United Church of Christ decided to address numerous building issues one step at a time. This friendly congregation also valued relationships and hospitality. They wanted a nice place to welcome people to their education program. One of their long-range goals is to spruce up the education building to make it look more like a church facility. They began the process with some simple steps. They replaced the old ceiling tiles with new ones, brightening and softening the look. They also repainted the building's common areas. Previously the bathrooms, halls, and fellowship hall all had a two-tone look with shiny green enamel paint on the bottom and a lighter, flat paint on the top. After painting, the rooms had one unifying soft blue color instead of each room having its own color. They also installed carpet and new baseboards throughout the educational portion and took down the old blackboards and cracked, marked, and crumbling bulletin boards and replaced them with new bulletin boards and white boards. They put furniture in the hall and added signs above each room so members and visitors can see what each room is. They also placed new mats in front of the doors

These functional improvements made the building more pleasing. People feel better about the place. And these positive feelings enhance their practice of hospitality. The practice of hospitality is also supported by the virtues of kindness and friendliness that the renovation inspires.

These three congregations dealt with different aesthetic issues related to an existing facility. They had to negotiate different feelings about tastes and the ways in which design shapes beliefs and behavior. They had to deal with the reality that space creates strong emotional connections that need to be honored or reassessed.

Your Aesthetic Issues

What are your aesthetic issues? How might you think about them? How, as you build or renovate, might you create beauty that inspires the virtues your congregation holds dear?

As you think about good design, you need to think in terms of your entire facility. Good design means that the sanctuary provides a positive feeling when you enter. It also means that the kitchen in the basement is not only functional, but has clear lines of traffic flow and is well organized. When making decisions about how your building should look, you can't limit your attention to just the worship space. Picture ways to make your entire facility beautiful.

Your sacred space team can improve the aesthetics of your facility. Trained resource persons, such as architects, designers, artists, interior designers, historical preservationists—ones with proven track records whom you can trust—can help. Make sure that those with whom you work understand the mission of your congregation so that the aesthetics of your building do not contradict your mission.

Though, in an ideal situation, you consider the whole building, the reality is that when you are renovating or restoring an existing building, you may work on just a portion of it. For Northview congregation it was the barn. The people at St. Joan of Arc selected their sanctuary. Zion United Church of Christ made changes to their educational facility. Regardless of what your project is, begin by gathering your team in a meeting room that is not in a part of the building you intend to renovate or restore. Invite team members to describe the space you are working on. Be specific. Don't say, "The ceiling is tall." Describe the tall ceiling. What color is it? How tall is it? What are its distinguishing marks? Listen and record. What do people mention? After the space has been thoroughly described, move the group to the space. Now have them describe it again. Does it match the previous description? What was left out? What doesn't line up? This exercise gets at the gaps between the imagined aesthetics and real aesthetics. Look at the gaps as spaces for improvement.

If your goal is to restore a facility, invite a resource person who knows what your kind of space was designed to make people do or feel to talk to your team. This is what St. Joan of Arc did when they invited the priest to speak about their Roman basilica sanctuary. Think of the loss they would have suffered by changing the transcendent, dreamy, tall ceiling into something it was not meant to be.

If your goal is to renovate a particular space, invite a resource person to talk to your leadership about how space influences people's behavior. Have them show you how the way a space is designed shapes actions and conversations. The "third place" ideals noted earlier (the good, great place) move people to conversation. Good conversation leads people to deeper relationships. If this is a goal for your renovation, invite someone knowledgeable about the aesthetics of a third place gathering area to speak to your group.

Whatever part of your building you are discussing, you must make carefully thought-out decisions regarding aesthetics, because the way a place looks makes a difference in the way people respond to God and to their neighbors. The way a building looks stirs feelings, positive or negative, about God and God's world. Father Richard Vosko writes: "It is safe to say that most people who belong to a faith tradition are searching for some kind of experience that will move them toward a better way of life. A life that is, in some way, holy and wholly other than what is being experienced now. This is the tremendous burden placed on religious architecture—to serve as a firm foundation of faith and a platform for courage and creativity."[10]

Summary for Your Team

- Know that aesthetics is more than a contest between tastes. A building with good aesthetics helps people act more fully human, better equipped with the virtues of their faith. Aesthetics is also code language for the way in which sacred space carries memories and connections.
- Discuss aesthetics from an ethic of respect for neighbor. You do not have to love what others love about a sacred space. But if you respect another point of view, your view is more easily heard.
- Aesthetics are too important to be left entirely to the professionals. They are also too important to be left entirely to nonprofessionals.

Questions for Your Team

1. What is your first memory of a sacred place? What was it like? What ideas did it communicate? What feelings did you have about it?
2. Look at photographs of other sacred places. Talk together about what values the images represent. This will help you

practice talking about your own space and your congregation's values.

3. Who can help you think theologically about what your space communicates? Theology and aesthetics are close cousins.

4. Are there some parts of your sacred space that are untouchable? That is, are there some spaces that the congregation is just not willing or ready to change?

5. What words will you choose to tell a resource person—an architect or designer—what it is that you want your building to convey? How will you check to see if the professional understood what you meant?

CHAPTER 5 What Approach to Building Will We Use?

Project Delivery

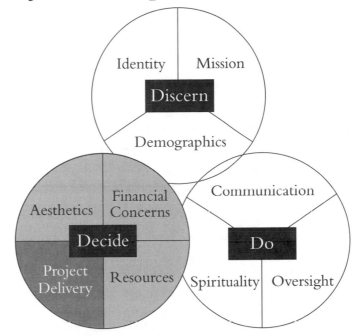

*S*uppose your family plans to travel from your home in the Midwest to California for a vacation. First, you have to decide how to get there. What are your options? Your choice is dependent on a number of factors. Do you have a fixed amount of money to spend on transportation? If so, you may choose the least expensive way. Or maybe your time is limited—you only have a week's vacation. In that case, speed may be the most important factor. Do you want to see the countryside? Perhaps you will choose the train so you can see the scenery and have access to a dining room and a sleeping room.

This also lets you avoid traffic and any need for lodging you would encounter driving across the country. Maybe part of the joy of travel for your family is unplanned side trips. You like turning off the main roads and exploring small towns. In that case, you will want to drive. Do you have children, and if so, what ages are they? What form of transportation works best for them? Would you like to travel in a motor home? Perhaps you could borrow or rent one.

In the same way that planning a vacation requires making decisions about how to get to your destination, so too, building projects require making decisions about getting from vision to occupancy of a remodeled, restored, or new facility. We call the different ways of getting from your envisioned facility to its realization "project delivery methods." Just as no one mode of transportation is best for every family, no project delivery method is right for every congregation. This chapter explores several project delivery methods and the advantages and disadvantages of each. As part of that exploration, we address the question "What approach to building will we use?" That is, what is your preferred project delivery method?

Project Delivery Methods

Bill Chegwidden, architect and author of *The Next Step: How to Discover the Right Solutions to Plan, Design, and Build Your Church*, describes five project delivery methods and their advantages and disadvantages.[1] We are using an adapted version of Chegwidden's five. If you are interested in other project delivery methods, please explore the project delivery resources found in appendix G. The *Handbook on Project Delivery*[2] is especially helpful in identifying the distinctions among the methods as well as the roles of the owner, builder, and designer in each method.

The five main methods we will look at are design-bid-build, negotiated select team,[3] design-build, construction management, and
package builder. The chart below summarizes the advantages and
disadvantages of each method.

PROJECT DELIVERY METHOD	DESCRIPTION	ADVANTAGES	DISADVANTAGES
Design-Bid-Build	The "traditional," linear approach. First architectural designs, then bid, then hire contractor.	• Owner can be attentive at all stages. • Best price can be selected from competitive bidding. • Three entities involved provides checks and balances. • Contractor bid based on complete design means more accurate cost estimate.	• Cost unknown until late in process. • Potential communication problems between architect and contractor. • Longer process than design-build. • No contract between architect and contractor.
Design-Build	Single firm does both the design and the build. Design-build firms do more expansion, new construction than remodeling projects.	• Communication is smoother because one firm is involved. • Congregation holds one contract. • Quicker than traditional design-bid-build. • Often less expensive than design-bid-build.	• Checks and balances eliminated. • Design and build phases overlap means less attention to both for congregation. • May be difficult to terminate contract between design and build stages without losing the design. • Early cost commitment may mean quality sacrifices to meet cost.

PROJECT DELIVERY METHOD	DESCRIPTION	ADVANTAGES	DISADVANTAGES
Negotiated Select Team	Contractor enters the process at the design phase rather than after design and bidding process.	• Contractor's budget expertise is used early in the process. • Team approach developed early. • Contractors can be selected for reputation and quality rather than lowest bidder. • Checks and balances of two contracts are maintained.	• If trust is lacking, team approach is hindered. • Some congregations feel early contractor selection eliminates competitive bidding. • Keeping design within budget is still difficult even with contractor participating in design phase.
Construction Management	Useful only for large, complex projects. Architect and contractor perform typical roles. Additional team member is the construction manager who plans, coordinates, and oversees the project.	• Relieves oversight and management responsibilities from congregation. • Serves as an owner's representative (see chapter 10).	• Adds complexity to communications. • Costs more for additional person. • Congregation has no direct communications with architect or builder.
Package Builder	Provides predesigned, pre-engineered, and manufactured buildings using template plans. A local architect is usually hired to make minor modifications in the plans.	• Competitive pricing. • Faster occupancy than other methods. • Early cost estimates. • Congregation has one contract.	• Few possibilities for design modification and creativity. • Architect works for company, not congregation.

Before delving into the descriptions of each delivery method, let's take a brief overview of the early historical development of the delivery methods. Doing so will help put the current methods into perspective.

Centuries ago a master builder constructed buildings. The master builder was responsible for designing and building a facility. Sometimes a master builder's role included making or overseeing the making of the furniture, as well. The master builder method continued as the predominate method into the industrial revolution and was sometimes used in the twentieth century.[4] But the predominate twentieth-century building method was the design-bid-build approach. After the move from the master building to the design-bid-build method, the other delivery modes named above developed over time. This multiplicity of project delivery options, like a shopper's choices at the grocery store, makes the decision-making and building processes more complex for congregations. Some project delivery methods discussed here are appropriate for all kinds of building projects, from new construction to historic restoration. Other project delivery methods are only applicable to new construction.

The terminology used for project delivery methods, other than the two most popular—design-bid-build and design-build—varies from architect to architect, builder to builder, and book to book. In your reading and research, you may discover different names for the methods we describe here. This is a good reminder that when your congregation explores project delivery methods, you need to ask what architects or builders mean by the terms they use.

Design–Bid–Build Definition

The traditional design-bid-build delivery method consists of hiring an architect to create a design for your new building or for expansion, renovation, or restoration of your existing space. After the congregation or its representatives have approved the design, contractors are invited to submit a bid detailing the cost they will charge to build what the architect designed. After reviewing the bids, the congregation chooses the firm they want to use. They then enter into a contract directly with that firm. The architect offers guidance in selecting an appropriate construction firm, but a congregation's choice of a contractor or specialty vendors is not limited to those recommended by the architect. Nevertheless, you are wise to consider the compatibility of the architect and builder, because the stress on the sacred space team, and ultimately the quality of the work, are largely dependent on the quality of the relationship and communication between the firms involved. While the construction firm is responsible for the actual building, the architect remains active in the process by ensuring that what was designed is being constructed the way it was meant to be built. The architect also conducts the final inspection of the completed facility.

Advantages of Design–Bid–Build

There are several advantages to the traditional design-bid-build project delivery method. The first is that it allows the owner to give full attention to each phase of the building project. Since the process is linear and sequential, the second of three phases (bid) does not begin until the first phase (design) is done. The building (third phase) doesn't begin until the bids are in and the best bid has been accepted. This linear process provides congregations with considerable input at each phase. A second advantage is that competitive bidding for the cost of construction or restoration lets a congregation compare costs and select a contractor who submits the bid they feel is best.

In the design-bid-build method, a congregation holds a contract with both the architect and the contractor. Since this project delivery involves three entities in the project—the owner/congregation, architect, and contractor—it provides a healthy system of checks and balances. A final advantage is that, since the contractors' bidding requires complete construction documents from the architect, the contractors are able to provide accurate cost commitments.

Disadvantages of Design–Bid–Build

Some of the advantages of a project delivery method can also be disadvantages. The linear nature of the design-bid-build method means that a congregation doesn't get an accurate feel for the cost until the project is sent out for bids. This can be problematic since congregations are frequently surprised by how much construction costs. The architect, while knowledgeable, doesn't have the expertise to provide realistic cost estimates. Costs are contractors' expertise. Since a contractor typically isn't hired until his or her bid is accepted, congregations frequently receive a budget surprise.

Another disadvantage of design-bid-build is that you have two different businesses, the architect and the construction firm, working on the same project, sometimes causing communication to be problematic. When a problem surfaces, the architect may claim it is the fault of the contractor, while the contractor may complain that the architect's design is flawed. Maintaining adequate communication between the architect and the contractor is a constant challenge in the design-bid-build method.

Another disadvantage is that the design-bid-build process is a longer process than some of the others. It is sequential. It is unlike the design-build method that is done by a single firm that can begin construction before a design is fully completed.

The final disadvantage is that there is no contract between the architect and the contractor. Instead, each holds an independent contract with the congregation. This means that if the architect visits the construction site and sees something that is not right, he or she has no authority over the contractor. The architect simply reports to the congregation what has been observed. Likewise, if the contractor discovers aspects of the design that won't work given any number of variables, he or she has no contractual way to address this issue with the architect.

Design–Build Definition

Design-build is the second most common project delivery method used today. A single firm doing both the design and the construction of a building or expansion characterizes this method. The congregation holds one contract rather than two. While design-build firms can do remodeling projects, typically they focus on new construction. Because the contractors are working on the project early on, the design-build firm makes an early cost commitment to the owner. This method compensates for some of the disadvantages of the design-bid-build method, but, as we will see, it has its own disadvantages.

Advantages of Design–Build

The advantages of the design-build method are many. It requires that the congregation hold only one contract, which reduces much of the potential for misunderstandings and communication problems between the architect and the builder because they both work for the same firm. And since one entity handles both the design and the building, construction can begin before the design is fully completed. This makes for a faster building process than the linear design-bid-build approach. Another advantage is that this method is often less expensive than the traditional approach because a congregation does not have to hire an independent architect.

Disadvantages of Design–Build

A congregation holding only one contract instead of two can be an advantage, but it can also be a disadvantage. Since the same firm does both the design and the building, the typical checks and balances that occur when two firms are involved are eliminated. Also, because some aspects of the design and construction phases are done simultaneously with a design-build approach, a congregation doesn't have as much involvement in each phase as it does when the phases are done one at a time. Some congregations have discovered challenges when they, for whatever reason, wanted to terminate their contract with the design-build firm after initial designs were provided. In this scenario, a congregation may lose the money it invested in the design-build firm's design because, due to contractual, copyright, or other issues, another builder often cannot build the design created by the original firm. In a design-build arrangement, the architect works for the design-build firm rather than for the congregation. The firm, not the congregation, then "owns" the building plans. The architect's main loyalty is to the design-build firm, not to the congregation.

Finally, since the design-build firm has made an early cost commitment, quality sacrifices may need to be made as the project progresses in order for the firm to stay within the promised budget.

Definition of Negotiated Select Team

To overcome some of the challenges inherent in the two most common building methods, some architectural firms use a method often called the negotiated select team. This approach requires that the construction firm be hired before the project is designed. The contractor attends and participates in all design meetings with the architect and congregation.

Advantages of Negotiated Select Team

A negotiated select team arrangement accomplishes several things. First, as a design emerges, the contractor can use his or her building expertise to project realistic costs. This enables the congregation to eliminate aspects of the design that it feels are beyond its budget. The second advantage to this approach is that a team—congregation/owner, architect, and contractor—is developed from the outset. Third, the congregation is able to select a contractor based on reputation for quality instead of based on the lowest bid. Fourth, the congregation still holds two contracts. It thereby avoids the perceived conflict of interest often cited as a disadvantage of the design-build method.

Disadvantages of Negotiated Select Team

As with any project delivery method, there are disadvantages to the negotiated select team. Though a team is formed from the beginning, the strength of the team is dependent on ongoing trust among its members. If at any point trust and cooperation wane, the process can break down quickly.[5]

Since the contractor is selected early on, congregations sometimes feel that they miss competitive bidding for the project. Some of this perceived disadvantage can be overcome by competitive bids by the subcontractors.

Even though a contractor is present to provide realistic costs as the design progresses, it is still difficult to keep the project on budget during the design phase.[6] That is due partly to fluctuations in building material costs over which the contractor has no control.

Definition of Construction Management

The construction management project delivery method consists of an owner hiring a construction manager to oversee the entire project. In this approach, the architect and contractor perform traditional roles. This method is useful for complex projects requiring a lot of planning, scheduling, and coordination.[7] It involves four players in the project—the owner, architect, contractor, and construction manager.[8]

Advantages of Construction Management

The prime advantage of the construction management method is that it provides a congregation with someone who oversees the building process. This is especially helpful for congregations who have neither the time nor the expertise to do so themselves. A construction manager plays a role similar to that of an owner's representative (see chapter 10). He or she carefully monitors the cost and schedule of the entire project.

Disadvantages of Construction Management

The primary disadvantage of the construction management method is that it means additional expenses for another player in the building process. Thus this method may not be practical for small to medium building projects. Another disadvantage is that, since the construction manager is the congregation's representative with the architect and contractor, the owner/congregation has no direct communication with either of those vendors. This involvement of a fourth entity in the project can lead to role confusion.

Definition of Package Builder

A package builder, like a design-builder, provides both architectural and construction services. A congregation chooses from a selection of primarily steel buildings that have already been developed for other worship spaces. These buildings are predesigned, pre-engineered, and manufactured before the construction process begins. The package builder typically hires a local architect to make minor alterations in the design to meet local codes or a congregation's desired changes. The exteriors of such buildings can be finished in a variety of ways, according to the desires of the congregation. An Internet search will help your congregation find providers of package buildings.

Advantage of Package Builder

The advantages of this method include competitive cost, faster occupancy than other methods, reliable and early cost limits, one contract for the congregation, and a clear building schedule.

Disadvantage of Package Builder

Once again, the advantages of a method can also be the disadvantages. In this case, since a congregation selects predesigned templates, it has few possibilities for any design creativity or uniqueness. Congregations that require considerable adjustments in the design will not realize the cost savings that are this method's primary appeal. Another possible disadvantage is that the architect works for the builder instead of the congregation.

Regardless of the project delivery method you choose, it is often helpful to have an attorney look at any contract with architects and builders or other vendors before you sign it.

The project delivery method your congregation selects depends on several important factors—the extent to which the congregation wants to be involved in the building project, the speed with which you need your facility built or renovated, the materials you want to be used, and the nature of your project. Are you building a new facility or adding new construction to an existing building? Renovating existing space? Restoring and preserving a historic building? Some project delivery methods are better suited to certain kinds of projects.

How can you figure out which delivery method is best for your congregation? Here are four suggestions that will aid in answering that question.

First, *learn the options*. Everybody on the building committee needs to know the basic project delivery options that are appropriate for the kind of project you are planning. It is not necessary for everybody to know the nuances of each approach, but each member needs to understand the broad characteristics of each and differences between them. Use this chapter to help inform the building team.

Second, *talk to other congregations*. Call other congregations who have recently completed a project similar to your own. Create a set of questions to ask on a visit to their facility. Take notes as you walk through their building. Talk to members of the congregation who served on the project. Ask them about their satisfaction with the project delivery method they used and what they would do differently.

Third, *interview professional representatives of both of the dominant methods*. Invite an architect and a representative from a design-build firm to come and talk with your building committee. Do this early in your building process. Ask them to talk about the project delivery method they represent and the advantages they think it possesses. Also, ask them to discuss some of the weaknesses of their method and their strategies for minimizing them.

Fourth, *assess your values*. A key to selecting a project delivery method appropriate for your congregation is the value you place on each one of the three key components of a building project: quality, time, and budget. Typically, a building project can deliver two of these key elements. It cannot deliver all three. Your building committee needs to ask, "Which of these three are most important to us?" Is it most important to have the project completed as quickly as possible? Within budget? Or to the highest possible standards? If you want the highest quality completed as quickly as possible, you will not be able to constrain costs. If you need to complete your project as quickly as possible to complete financing at a particular rate or to occupy the facility at a certain date, you will have to make some sacrifices in the cost and/or the quality.

Selecting the project delivery method you feel is best for your congregation is not the only factor in a successful building project. The Project Delivery Institute has identified three other crucial keys to having a successful building project regardless of the project delivery method used:

- Preparing a knowledgeable, trustworthy, and decisive facility owner/congregation.
- Assembling a team with relevant experience and good chemistry as early as possible. This must happen before 20 percent of the project design is completed.
- Signing a contract that encourages and rewards the organizations for behaving as a team.[9]

In most congregational building projects that require outside assistance, the sacred space team will have a choice to make about which project delivery method to use. An awareness of the methods useful for your project and the advantages and disadvantages of each will enable your team and others in your congregation to make wise choices that ensure the success of your project.

Summary for Your Team

- Project delivery methods are ways a congregation gets from a vision of a new or renovated facility to its realization.
- The two most common project delivery methods are design-bid-build and design-build.
- Additional delivery methods include negotiated select team, construction management, and packaged builders. These methods are sometimes referred to by different terms.
- Each project delivery method has advantages and disadvantages.
- To select the project delivery method for you, learn the options, talk to others, interview professionals, and assess the priority of your values—time, quality, or budget.

Questions for Your Team

1. How will you learn more about the different project delivery methods and their advantages and disadvantages?
2. What project delivery methods are appropriate for your building project?
3. Do you know the project delivery method preferred by the architects/builders in your area? If not, do you have

team members who are willing to do some homework on this?

4. At this point in your building planning, what does your sacred space team feel is the primary value of your congregation—budget, speed, or quality? What evidence do you have for your impression? Are there other members of your congregation you might invite to join your sacred space team for a discussion of these values? Who are they and when could that discussion be scheduled?

CHAPTER 6 What Service Providers
Will We Use?

Resources

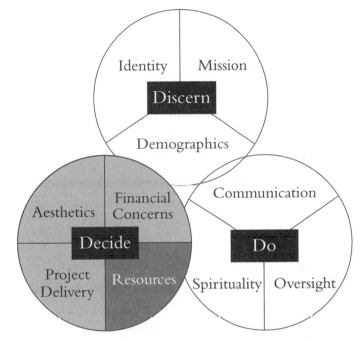

*A*t an open house for a recently completed building for a new
church plant, the architect and contractor joined members of the
building committee in leading tours of the facility. The congregation
exuded pride at achieving this milestone. Following the tour, the
contractor and the congregation's building committee chairperson
talked privately with some remaining visitors. It was obvious to the
listeners that there was a great deal of mutual respect between the
contractor and chairperson. The contractor had blessed the congregation not only by the quality of his work, but also by communicating

frequently and being sensitive to the congregation's needs. The building committee chairperson had been a constant presence during the building process. They each praised the role of the other. This good fit of builder and building committee ensured that the congregation's project was both successful and fulfilling.

The careful selection of resources is the third "decision" in the decide phase of the discern, decide, do model. Earlier elements in this phase included decisions about aesthetics (chapter 4) and project delivery (chapter 5).

Congregations doing any building project, whether it is renovation, restoration, expansion, or new construction, must make wise use of a wide variety of resources—persons, businesses, firms, vendors, materials, consultants, books, videos, or other things needed to move a project from start to finish. The service providers or resources that a congregation chooses to use make a crucial difference in the quality of the final facility and the quality of the entire process.

As we consider the resources that building projects require, we will begin with learning resources—books, DVDs, other congregations, and building professionals, anything or anyone from which your team can learn about the issues that need to be addressed in your building project. Following learning resources, we will discuss how to find appropriate vendors and how to select architects and builders. Finally, we will explore using volunteers in your building project.

Start with Learning

A 120-year-old congregation was bursting the seams of their building and needed to expand, so they formed a building committee. Because this was a significant committee in the congregation's life, the president of the governing board was appointed chairperson of the building committee. He admitted that neither he nor anyone else selected to serve on the building committee had any experience with or knowledge of building projects. He knew the team had a lot to learn. A congregation down the road from the first one filled its building committee with engineers, architects, and construction managers. Their sacred space team had extensive experience with building projects. Whether your building committee members have extensive, some, or no experience with building projects, it is important for the committee to take intentional time and effort for learning before embarking on their important task. Engaging in learning together creates a common experience for all team members. It also produces a level playing field for all the participants.

We have all heard that experience is the best teacher. Fast-growing congregations moving from one building project to another are in a position to apply experience from previous projects to current ones. But most congregations do not have that luxury. Few congregations go through major building projects more than once per generation, so each new building committee doesn't have the benefit of learning from the previous generation's team. Thus there is potential for making mistakes. So how can they intentionally learn what a building project involves and therefore avoid common mistakes?

That's where learning resources come in. It is often best to begin with books or other media that provide a broad overview of the congregational building process (see appendix G). In that way you will have some basic knowledge prior to meeting with building professionals.

One such resource is the Indianapolis Center for Congregations' DVD titled *Sacred Space: Discern, Decide, Do*.[1] This DVD was produced to be helpful to congregations of a wide variety of faith traditions. It presents the sacred space model that is used in this book and features congregations talking about what they learned while going through

> Learning resources are resources used for the specific pur-
> pose of learning about congregational building ventures.
> Learning resources include things such as the following:
>
> - books
> - media
> - consultants
> - other congregations
> - building professionals
> - Web sites

their building project. Sacred space teams can use this DVD in several ways. One way is to show one segment (there are nine on the DVD) to the sacred space team during each meeting. Each segment leads to a discussion using questions provided in the accompanying study guide. Another way to use the DVD is to show and discuss one of the phases—discern, decide, or do—at one meeting. Another approach is to order multiple copies of the DVD and ask members to watch specific segments at home in preparation for discussing them at the next team meeting. You may also find it helpful to show parts of the DVD to your governing body or to the entire congregation.

Of course, the Indianapolis Center's DVD is just one of numerous resources available. Many denominations provide resources to enable their congregations to learn about building processes. *Built of Living Stones: Art, Architecture, and Worship*[2] contains the guidelines of the United States Conference of Catholic Bishops for building and/or renovating Roman Catholic churches. This book contains guidance for theological reflection as well as a description of the practical aspects of a building project. An excellent online resource for Reform Judaism on synagogue building projects is *Rejoice in Your Handiwork: Sacred Space and Synagogue Architecture*.[3] Even if your congregation is not Roman Catholic or Jewish, you may find these resources helpful. Though *Rejoice in Your Handiwork* is written for Reform Jews, congregations of other faith traditions will find much of it adaptable and helpful for their context. For example, appendix 1 of part 1 offers a "Checklist of Things to Consider and Things to Do" that is useful for building projects of any faith tradition.

Some denominational Web sites offer planning documents that describe things to consider when building certain kinds of space, such as education or worship spaces. Two examples are the Disciples of Christ's (Christian Church) planning guides[4] and the FACTSheets provided by the Baptist General Conference of Texas.[5] You will want to explore what building-related resources are offered by your denomination or other congregational connections. Does your larger faith community offer web links that would be helpful in introducing you to building projects?

In addition to videos, DVDs, and online articles, there are a number of books that offer helpful insights. One especially helpful resource, introduced in the previous chapter, is Bill Chegwidden's book *The Next Step: How to Discover the Right Solutions to Plan, Design, and Build Your Church*.[6] This book is expensive but is very useful for both its comprehensiveness and its beautiful illustrations of exterior and interior places of worship. The nature of the work you plan to do will determine what books will be useful to your congregation.

There are many creative ways to use books as learning resources. You may choose to have copies of a particular title for your entire sacred space team so that everyone can read and then discuss it. Or you may ask one or two people on your team to read a book, present its salient information, and then lead a discussion. No matter how you use a book, the focus needs to be on what the resource offers that will help you in the building process. Some books will be useful as references throughout your entire sacred space project.

The Indianapolis Center for Congregations has developed a free downloadable resource titled *Beyond Reading: Using Books as Resources*[7] that offers suggestions about how congregational groups can make effective use of books.

Besides resources such as books and media to be used within your congregation, there are learning resources outside of your congregation. These include other congregations and professional architects and builders. Other congregations are superb learning resources. By visiting them, you can make observations about the design and materials used by particular architects and builders. By talking to their building committees, you can learn what mistakes they made and how to avoid them. You can talk to them about what project delivery system they used, how they made that choice, and whether in hindsight they would do it differently. Many times, by talking to other congregations, you can discover aspects of a building project that you may not learn about any other way—such as what they did with the day care when their facility was being renovated.

So how do you find congregations that have something to teach you? Perhaps you have driven by a relatively new place of worship and thought it attractive. Or you may have seen on potential architects' Web sites some pictures of their work on places of worship. Maybe you know people from other congregations that have expanded, renovated, or built new facilities. These are just a few of the many ways of developing a list of congregations you would like to contact. Once you have identified congregations you would like to visit, set up an appointment with the chair of the building committee or with someone who worked on the committee.

Know in advance what you want to learn from the congregations you contact. Your focus may be directed to examining the final product—the design of the space, the quality of the work, and the materials used. If so, look to see if the finished design and product are compatible with what you envision for your congregation. This visual inspection will help you learn whether you are interested in considering the architect and/or builder of the space you are visiting.

If, on the other hand, your primary purpose is to learn more about the building process, ask questions such as: What was the nature of your project? What service providers did you use and why? What was your experience? What did you learn? Describe a snag and how it was resolved. Although it is likely that you want to learn several things from a congregation, unless you are intentional about what it is you want to learn, you may overlook other valuable insights that you could have gleaned.

Building professionals are learning resources that are sometimes overlooked. Many architects, builders, and capital fund consultants are willing to spend an hour or so with a congregation explaining the services their firm provides. Though they may look upon such a visit as customer cultivation, your congregation can use it as a learning experience. The difference is in the questions that your congregation is prepared to ask the expert. When learning from professionals, as opposed to discussing a potential contract, ask questions related to the field they represent. Ask them the most important thing you need to consider as you select a firm offering their kind of professional services. Have them tell you about a time when their work with a congregation went as well as it possibly could. What made it so successful? Then have them tell about a time when the project fell apart. What happened? These "learning" meetings serve two functions: (1) they provide your sacred space team an opportunity to learn more about the field of design, building, or funding; and (2) they enable your congregation to assess whether the services of the professionals you interview could be a match for your congregation.

While you could do this learning with any architect or other professional, it will be most meaningful if you have such a conversation with someone you are interested in hiring for your project. In fact, the most important decisions your sacred space team may make are selecting the right professionals for the design, building, and funding aspects of your project. For example, if you are restoring a historic synagogue, you will not want to visit with an architect who builds only new churches. Similarly, if you want new construction that focuses more on function than on form, you will not want to meet with an architect specializing in historic restoration.

Select Professional Resources

There are several steps to selecting professional resources—architects, builders, fund consultants, and so forth to work on your building project. First is discovery—finding a pool of potential professionals. During this phase you compile a broad but limited list. It is limited in the sense that you don't want so many names on the list that it becomes unwieldy. Ways to discover potential vendors include searching the web for professionals in your region, consulting with your denominational leaders, finding out whom other congregations in your area have used, and having conversations with friends who may have some knowledge or experience. Searching the Web sites of professional organizations is also a good idea. Often they have directories of their members.[8]

After compiling your original list, your sacred space team will want to weed out all but three or four serious contenders. Trying to explore a larger list of serious potential vendors in-depth is too complex, confusing, and inefficient. Moving from compiling a list of potential resources to selecting the professionals you feel best fit your needs and relate well with your sacred space team is a process that takes time and intentionality.

The quality and cost of the architect's and builder's work are not the only things to consider when selecting professionals for your project. Other considerations include how easy they are to work with, how clear and timely their communications are with congregational representatives, how they stayed on schedule and on budget with previous projects, how they handled unexpected developments, and so forth. That's where the congregational visits mentioned earlier really help. Ask questions as you visit to uncover your own sense of these factors.

A congregation's standards for selecting building profession-als need to include both some common criteria and some criteria important to your unique congregation. Common criteria include quality work, communication skills, honesty, and integrity. Unique criteria may include availability to meet your congregation's time frame and design requirements, workmanship that matches your congregation's needs, relational connection to your congregation's team, and the like.

When selecting the key vendors for your building project, your sacred space team must develop a decision-making process. One congregation in our area began by determining the questions they wanted to ask architects and design-build firms. They then divided up the names of eight to ten local firms and had different members of their team make phone calls asking for the identical information. Then someone on the team created a matrix showing each firm and the responses that were given (see last page of appendix C). This enabled the team to quickly review the information, eliminate those they felt were not suited to their needs, and pursue the others.

Another congregation created a detailed interview guide for use with perspective architects. The guide enabled members of their sacred space team to rate the prospect on a scale of 1 to 10. The scores were compiled and then used to assist the team in making their decision. What they discovered was that all the firms were high on some factors and lower on others. This made the scores fairly close. In light of that, their choice came down to the one they thought was most compatible with their sacred space team.

These are two examples of intentional processes that helped congregations avoid several common pitfalls when selecting facility-related vendors. One pitfall is the temptation to select a vendor related to someone in the congregation. A mainline congregation we worked with recently hired a relative of a governing board member to fix its leaky roof. Soon the repaired roof began to leak. They didn't know how to handle this, so they didn't. Afraid of hurting the feelings of the board member who had recommended his brother, they ignored the problem—until, that is, it could be ignored no longer. The leak damaged the sanctuary. Although there may be times when it is fine to hire a member of the congregation or relative of a member, this should never be done without a bidding process, along with bonding and certificates of insurance, which the member submits like other interested firms.

A second pitfall for congregational teams is leaning toward a vendor who has charisma or an impressive presentation. Make sure that vendors have competency and ability, not just charm or persuasiveness.

A third pitfall is recency bias. Sometimes sacred space teams are drawn to the most recent person they interviewed because their memory of that person is fresher than their memories of early presenters.

When selecting architects or design-build firms to guide you through your building project, make certain that they have the appropriate credentials. Various professions have standards that vendors must meet to be certified in that profession. The national professional organization for architects is the American Institute of Architects. The AIA Web site will help you locate certified AIA architects in your region of the country.[9]

Besides national or regional accreditation, be sure to check your potential vendor's local knowledge. Ask them how they keep abreast of your community's current building codes. This is crucial. We know a congregation that engaged an architect to build an addition to their existing facility. They assumed that this architect, who had come highly recommended from other congregations, knew about local building codes. The architect's failure to check the local building codes to ensure that the congregation's addition was code compliant led to a two-month delay and the need for a zoning variance request. The congregation reported that "it was very upsetting!"

A major criteria in selecting a contractor to work on your building project is that the firm is licensed and carries adequate insurance. The Associated General Contractors of America[10] recommends that you verify a contractor's licenses, make sure the firm has at least five years of experience, and then contact the Better Business Bureau to see if it has any information on the firm. Your local municipal building department or metropolitan building association should be able to tell you if a contractor has the proper licenses to work on your project. Brotherhood Mutual Insurance Company,[11] a group that works with many congregations, recommends that all contractors and subcontractors submit a certificate of insurance. Insurance coverage should include worker's compensation and vehicle and liability coverage. We also recommend that you ask for builders' risk insurance that will cover damage to the structure or materials incurred during the construction phase. If the contractor does not have that kind of insurance, your congregation may want to purchase coverage through your insurance company.

Use Volunteers

Now that we have explored a variety of professionals as resources, let's turn to considering volunteers as resources. Some denominations have teams of construction volunteers who build, renovate, or remodel churches. Typically the volunteers are retirees who are free to travel and provide their own transportation and expenses. Many groups consist of both skilled and unskilled workers. Some teams are organized primarily to build the first building for a new church plant. Other teams do that and also volunteer for building projects of established churches. Some denominations can pull together a complete construction team to do an entire building project. The Southern Baptist Convention calls their volunteer construction program Baptist Builders. Baptist Builders helps with planning, construction, and occupancy. Their Web site offers many helpful resources.[12] Laborers for Christ[13] is the Lutheran Church–Missouri Synod group. It helps Missouri Synod congregations build churches, parsonages, and parish halls and does remodeling. Other denominations blend construction volunteer recruitment into a wider category of volunteers for many different kinds of volunteer mission work. They advertise the special skills that are needed on particular projects. The projects and appropriate volunteers are then connected. The Cooperative Baptist Fellowship uses this model.[14]

In addition to outside volunteer construction teams, some congregations invest considerable volunteer hours to help build their own place of worship. Such an endeavor requires several crucial components. First is a contractor who is committed to working with volunteers and supervising them in such a way that the entire project is coordinated and completed with quality. Second is a congregation member who serves as a liaison with the contractor and matches tasks with volunteers. Third are volunteers who have the flexibility and willingness to complete their work when it is needed and in a timely manner. Fourth is clarity about whether the congregation intends to use only skilled volunteers or to use unskilled volunteers as well.

Marilyn McClellan, member of First Congregational United Church of Christ in Bellingham, Washington, tells the story of the church volunteers who saved their congregation considerable money by donating more than six thousand volunteer hours. Professionals did the biggest technical jobs, such as the foundation, electrical installations, dry wall completion, and so forth. Volunteers sorted bricks, sealed concrete, insulated pipes, cleaned the worksite, and did other such jobs. Skilled volunteers cleared the building site, installed the plumbing, created wood carvings, and did the landscaping.[15]

Congregations considering using volunteer laborers, whether from an outside team of construction volunteers or volunteers within their own congregation, need to explore the advantages and disadvantages of doing so. One good way to do this is to talk to congregations who have used this approach. If you want to use congregational volunteers, you need to select a contractor who has experience guiding a project using volunteers. Finally, your insurance company needs to be consulted to make sure that all volunteer laborers are adequately covered.

As you can see, there are many issues to think about as you consider the appropriate resources and service providers for your building project. Choosing the right fit for your congregation is a key act of the decide phase of the sacred space model. Regardless of what resources you choose, you will want to be thoughtful and intentional. This takes time. But these are decisions worth making carefully.

Summary for Your Team

- Congregational building projects require resources—books, media, other congregations, building professionals, fund consultants, and sometimes volunteers.
- Most congregational sacred space teams lack experience working on building projects and therefore need to be intentional about learning from resources.
- Other congregations are valuable resources from which sacred space teams can learn.
- Selection of major building professionals—designers, builders, and fund consultants—requires a deliberate selection process.
- If the contractor is willing and the congregation has appropriate supervision and organizational skills, volunteer labor can be a resource for a congregational building project.

Questions for Your Team

1. Discuss where you are currently in your building project. Have you already used some resources? What are they? How did you decide to use them?
2. What kinds of additional resources do you anticipate using?
3. What congregations in your area might you want to visit? Why?
4. What will your goal be when you are visiting the congregations you named?
5. When and how will your team work to develop a selection process for choosing an architect? Contractor? Fund consultant?

6. Have you previously used volunteers on a building project? If so, how did that work for your congregation?

CHAPTER 7 What Sources of Funding
Will We Use?

Financial Concerns

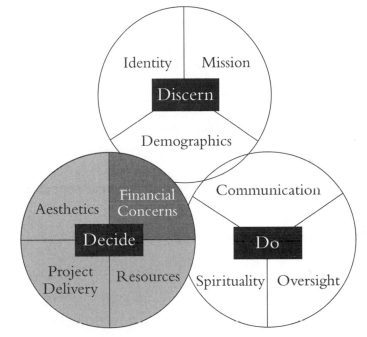

A new, rapidly growing congregation has outgrown their existing space in a shopping mall. It is time to relocate. They purchase land for a new building but are surprised at how much money it will take to develop the site. How will they fund this large, unanticipated expense?

Another congregation, meeting in a historic urban building, has allowed their stained-glass windows to deteriorate. Some pieces of glass are missing. A group in the congregation has spearheaded an attempt to repair and restore the windows. After getting quotes from four firms, they are shocked at the cost. It is far more than their budget can withstand. Where will they find the money to do the restoration?

These congregations and many others face the daunting task of raising money to pay for facility improvements and expansion. Funding is one of the most challenging aspects of building because facility projects typically demand resources beyond most congregational annual budgets.

In our work with congregations, the Indianapolis Center for Congregations has discovered the implementation of creative as well as traditional approaches to raising money for building projects. In this chapter we will review typical building project costs that need to be considered by congregations; explore ways of discovering how much a congregation can afford; discuss traditional capital campaigns, both those led by outside capital fund consultants and those led by members of the congregation; and share creative ways congregations have raised funds for their building projects.

In most congregations the sacred space team, or building committee, isn't the group responsible for raising the funds for the building project. Typically that role goes to an existing or specially created team. As in the case of the sacred space team, the finance team operates within the governing structure of the congregation and is accountable to the governing board.

Project Costs

It is not uncommon for congregations to experience cost surprises in the course of a building project. That is due partly to failure to consider all of the potential expenses. Such surprises can be minimized by thinking through all of the potential costs, including some that are frequently overlooked. Another factor is project overruns—budgeted expenditures such as building materials that cost more than anticipated. Hurricane Katrina, for instance, dramatically impacted the cost of wood. Overruns can be addressed by building contingencies into your project budget.

Before we look at ways of funding building projects, let's examine the common costs that congregations incur. Although this is not a comprehensive list of expenses, it contains both obvious expenditures and some that are often forgotten.

- architect and engineers for a conditions assessment in the case of expansion or renovation of existing space
- master plan
- land purchase
- site development, sometimes including utilities to the site
- architectural fees
- building contractors
- owner's representative
- fundraising consultant
- signage
- furnishings
- increased custodial services when expanding the size of the building(s)
- security improvements
- parking lots and amenities such as lighting
- landscaping
- increased cost of lawn care and snow removal
- increased utility costs

Not every project will have all these expenses. They are important enough, though, that congregations need to review them and ask whether they will be part of their particular project. We know more than one congregation that experienced disappointment and considerable delays, for example, because they failed to consider the cost of site development. They looked at the bricks and mortar and plaster and forgot about sewer lines.

One way to count the true cost of a project is to distinguish between the project cost and the construction cost. Construction cost is the amount required to build, or construct, the facility. It is much lower than the cost of the total project. Project cost, on the other hand, includes not only construction expenses, but also all additional expenses from land purchase to furniture. It also includes all costs required to complete and maintain the facility. Many congregations mistakenly assume that the construction cost represents the total amount required. In reality, the total project can cost as much as 30 to 50 percent more than the construction costs.[1]

Still, construction costs are the bulk of the expenditures. Congregations wanting to get a rough estimate of their construction cost (not project cost) can consult an online cost estimator such as Means QuickCost Estimator or McGraw Hill Commercial Construction Cost Estimator.[2] Both of these estimators are free. You do have to register to use them. To use them you begin by entering the number of square feet you are planning to build. Rough estimates of how much square footage is required for certain kinds of space—worship, fellowship, education—are available on several Web sites. Church Extension, a program of the Christian Church (Disciples of Christ) posts a variety of building program guides.[3] These include guides for worship space, Christian education space, administration space, and more. Each guide details the amount of square footage needed for each kind of building use. Another site, from the Baptist General Conference of Texas, offers a series of FACTSheets that detail required space based on usage.[4] Finally, Bill Chegwidden's *The Next Step* provides an extensive list of space usage square footage requirements.[5] Although these resources provide square footage guidelines for churches, synagogues will also find them applicable.

Using square foot guidelines for space usage and cost estimators for total square feet will give a congregation a rough estimate of their construction costs. To estimate your project costs, add 30 to 50 percent to your estimated construction cost. Remember, these figures are solely for the purpose of an initial estimate. Don't use them to define a project's actual cost. You need the assistance of professional architects and builders to arrive at "real" numbers. Still, these tools will give you a general idea of what kind of funding you will need.

Beyond your anticipated project cost, congregations need to reflect and make decisions about other expenditures. You will want to ensure funding for ongoing maintenance and repair of your newly built, restored, or renovated building(s). Congregational properties, like homes, require expenditures for ongoing maintenance and periodic replacement and updating. It is highly recommended that congregations determine a certain percentage of the amount they raise to be put in a restricted fund to be used solely for future building expenses. It is shortsighted and disappointing when congregations invest a lot of money to do projects, such as restoring their sanctuary to its original look, only to fail to maintain it due to lack of funds.

Another important consideration for congregations raising significant funds for their building is to revisit their mission. Doing so may well prompt your congregation to do something such as tithing the amount of money you raise for your own building and giving it to a congregation struggling to maintain their facility so they can use it to meet human needs. A congregation serving in one of the poorest areas of Indianapolis was able to build a family life center from which to serve the poor largely due to the financial contributions of a large congregation who chose to give from their abundance. Both allotments for maintenance and tithes for others will impact the amount you intend to raise.

How Much Can We Afford?

In addition to knowing the kinds of expenses they can expect to incur, congregations need to figure out how much they can afford. The first step is to evaluate your assets. This includes reviewing your current debt, any amount in your building fund, excess funds from your annual budget, and endowment funds that may be accessible and used for building projects. You will also want to consider other assets that can be liquidated to fund your building project. For example, a small congregation with whom the Center for Congregations worked sold a number of acres of property that had been given to them. The proceeds from the sale helped fund a much needed capital improvement on their building.

The next big question concerns debt. A congregation's attitude toward assuming debt also affects how much it can afford. If your congregation is willing to assume debt, there are guidelines for how much debt it is wise to incur. Many experts hold that a congregation should allot no more than 25 to 35 percent of their annual undesignated income to go to debt retirement.[6] Generally, financial institutions will loan two to three times the congregation's annual budget.[7]

Another way of considering how much you might borrow is by calculating the debt-to-value ratio. To do this, you divide the amount to be borrowed into the amount the property is worth. The resulting percentage gives you the debt-to-value ratio. Less than 60 percent debt-to-value ratio is conservative, 60 to 85 percent is aggressive, and 85 to 100 percent is risky.[8]

Considering your current assets and assessing the amount you are able to borrow are two ways of discovering how much your congregation can afford. But ultimately, the way you answer, "How much can we afford?" will be shaped by the fundraising strategies you decide to use.

Beyond establishing a sense of how much you can afford, you also need to determine when your congregation will consider its financial capacity. Do you do it before hiring an architect or design-build firm or after the conceptual architectural drawings? Or do you first engage in a fundraising initiative to see how much is raised? Each time frame has advantages and disadvantages. Not considering your financial capacity prior to hiring an architect means it is possible that the preliminary architectural design will call for funding exceeding the congregation's capacity. We know a congregation whose architect, based on what the congregation said they wanted and needed, produced a plan that would cost six million dollars to build. The congregation realized they could not afford more than three million. They had the building redesigned. In the process, though, they lost money, time, and the excitement and energy they had invested in the first plan.

On the other hand, evaluating your financial capacity before a vision is articulated and some visual expression of it is created also has its limitations. An architect's preliminary drawing of a new or renovated space motivates givers/pledgers far more than a general appeal to fund the idea of a new education wing. Congregants tend to give more to a project that has been visually presented to them.

Assessing your congregation's financial capacity on the results of a fundraising campaign held before a building project is defined is potentially limiting as well. Once again, people give/pledge more to specific projects than general building needs.

Weigh the advantages and disadvantages of each of the different times suggested for guesstimating your financial capacity. Which do you think is best for you? It may be best to intentionally review your financial capacity at different times throughout your entire project so that appropriate adjustments may be made.

Capital Campaigns

Once your congregation has identified the kinds of expenses it is likely to incur and established a general sense of what it can afford, it is ready to decide what strategies to use to raise the necessary funds. One of the most frequently used strategies is the capital campaign. A capital campaign is a pledge-driven fundraising effort to get larger sums of money than are available through a congregation's annual operating budget. Gifts to a capital campaign are intended to be over and above what members and friends already give to their congregation. Typically, those pledging to a capital campaign have three or five years to completely pay their pledge. A common rule of thumb says that a congregation can usually raise pledges of one and a half to two times the amount of their annual undesignated income in a three-year capital campaign. It can expect to receive 90 percent of the amount pledged.[9]

Many capital campaigns begin with a feasibility study. Such a study determines if the time is right to raise money for the proposed project, the degree of interest from potential donors, and the approximate amount the congregation can expect to raise. One benefit of using an outside fundraising consultant is that he or she has the tools and knowledge to conduct a feasibility study. Among aspects to be assessed during a thorough feasibility study are potential donors' perceptions of needs that will be met by the proposed project, statistics from the congregation (i.e., participating members, average worship attendance, annual operating budget, number of giving units), existing giving patterns of prospective donors, recent capital campaigns, the local economy, and conflict in the congregation. This list is illustrative but not comprehensive. Your study may cover more things.

You need to know, however, that the methods and thoroughness with which consultants perform feasibility studies vary greatly. When investigating and selecting a capital campaign consultant, your congregation must ask what procedures the consultant will use to conduct your feasibility study.

Once you have addressed issues related to feasibility, your team is ready to take the next steps. The next steps in traditional capital campaigns include creating a case statement, articulating the financial goal, identifying potential donors, asking for gifts, and celebrating the campaign's success.

A case statement explains clearly and succinctly why the project is needed, what it will achieve, and how it will further the mission of your congregation. It needs to include all of the reasons why giving to this cause is important to the donors.

Along with a case statement, donors need to know how much money the campaign seeks to raise. A reasonable financial goal both motivates and stretches givers. It generates enthusiasm by measuring success. Because falling short of a goal is defeating, it is important that the goal be realistically based on the giving capacity of the congregation. Whether the financial goal is one hundred thousand dollars or one million dollars, having a goal is more motivating than soliciting "however much we can raise."

Church Extension has a planning guide on their Web site that offers guidelines for determining appropriate ranges for capital campaign goals.[10] Of course, you need to know that formulas do not take into consideration intangibles—things such as donor belief in and commitment to the project or levels of conflict in the congregation.

Some congregations choose to establish two goals—a realistic one and one that requires stretching. The rationale for this is that achieving a goal is an excellent donor motivator, but making it too low is counterproductive.

Capital campaigns are not just organized around a goal or need. They need a theme. The theme conveys the tone of the message. Themes vary from sacrificial giving to "Blessed to be a blessing" to "See what great things the Lord can do for us." Selection of a capital campaign theme must fit your congregation's culture. While emphasis on sacrificial giving may be a great motivator in some congregations, others may find it distasteful.

A crucial factor in a successful capital campaign is the identifying of potential donors. Congregations often think exclusively of their members and friends as donors. That can be short-sighted. Partners for Sacred Places, a national not-for-profit organization based in Philadelphia, works with historic churches and synagogues to fund restoration projects.[11] They encourage congregations to think beyond their own membership. Sacred Places urges them to look at others who have an interest in a congregation's facilities. These may include former members—people who were active at one time but have moved away or the children of former clergy persons. In an exercise Sacred Places staffers Robert Jaeger and Tuomi Forest led for our sacred space project, they encouraged participants to think about who might have an interest in their building. One congregation realized that the oldest Boy Scout troop in their community had met in their church since it was founded twenty-five years before. They wondered if some former Boy Scouts and their families might have memories of the church that would prompt them to give toward its renovation.

Congregations can also broaden their perspective beyond individuals by considering donations from businesses and foundations. Partners for Sacred Places has created a resource, *Your Sacred Place Is a Community Asset: A Tool Kit to Attract New Resources and Partners,*[12] that guides congregations through an assessment of the worth of their services to the community. Congregations that offer food pantries, senior groups, day care, and so forth can calculate the dollar amount these services provide the community. Based on that information, they can approach businesses and foundations for donations to support the upkeep and expansion of the facilities housing these services.

Levels of Giving

In addition to identifying people or organizations with enough interest in giving, traditional capital campaign principles suggest that fundraisers identify the level of giving for those donors. A table of gifts, also called a pyramid of gifts (not a pyramid scheme!), is created in traditional capital campaigns. Basically, the pyramid divides the total financial goal of the campaign into the number of gifts that are required at different giving levels. Few large gifts are required to meet the goal, while a lot of smaller gifts are needed. A traditional rule of thumb for the pyramid of gifts is that the top gift needs to be 10 percent of the total goal, and the top ten gifts need to contribute one-third of the goal. The next one hundred gifts should make up another third of the goal, while the remaining gifts provide the final third.

More recently the traditional "rule of thirds" has been adapted to a "rule of the specific situation." The latter indicates the importance of each capital campaign creating a pyramid of gifts that reflects the capacity of their unique donors. Illustrations of the pyramid of gifts are found on pages 124 and 125. This method requires that those leading the campaign identify those who are likely to be able to give at the highest levels. All donors should be asked personally for a specific amount that the campaign leaders feel is within their capacity to make.

Standard Pyramid of Gifts

The Standard Pyramid of Gifts below is based on the traditional "Rule of Thirds" for a campaign with a $1,000,000 goal.

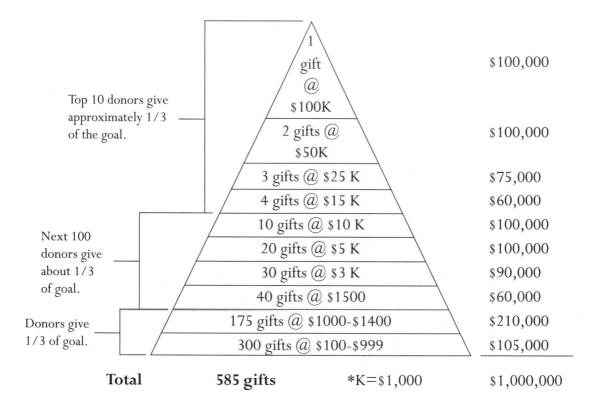

Top 10 donors give approximately 1/3 of the goal.	1 gift @ $100K	$100,000
	2 gifts @ $50K	$100,000
	3 gifts @ $25 K	$75,000
	4 gifts @ $15 K	$60,000
Next 100 donors give about 1/3 of goal.	10 gifts @ $10 K	$100,000
	20 gifts @ $5 K	$100,000
	30 gifts @ $3 K	$90,000
	40 gifts @ $1500	$60,000
Donors give 1/3 of goal.	175 gifts @ $1000-$1400	$210,000
	300 gifts @ $100-$999	$105,000
Total	**585 gifts** *K=$1,000	$1,000,000

Adapted from Peggy Powell Dean and Susanna A. Jones, *The Complete Guide to Capital Campaigns for Historic Churches and Synagogues.* Philadelphia, PA: Partners for Sacred Places, 1998, 21-22.

Modified Pyramid of Gifts

The Modified Pyramid of Gifts below is based on the "Rule of the Specific Situation" for a congregation with a capacity for three large gifts.

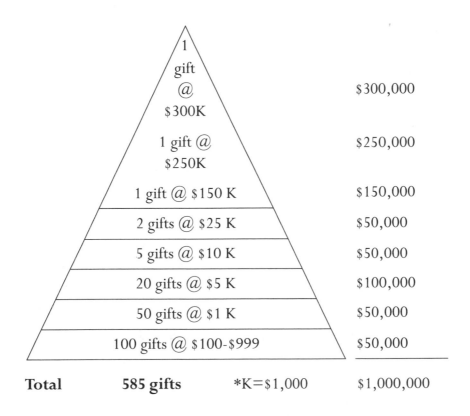

1 gift @ $300K			$300,000
1 gift @ $250K			$250,000
1 gift @ $150 K			$150,000
2 gifts @ $25 K			$50,000
5 gifts @ $10 K			$50,000
20 gifts @ $5 K			$100,000
50 gifts @ $1 K			$50,000
100 gifts @ $100-$999			$50,000
Total	**585 gifts**	*K=$1,000	$1,000,000

Adapted from Peggy Powell Dean and Susanna A. Jones, *The Complete Guide to Capital Campaigns for Historic Churches and Synagogues.* Philadelphia, PA: Partners for Sacred Places, 1998, 21-22.

Once potential donors have been identified, they need to be asked to give. That way they can hear the goals of the campaign and be asked directly for a contribution. One of the biggest downfalls of capital campaigns is not asking donors directly for a gift. People like to be valued sufficiently that their gifts are personally solicited. While many capital campaign consultants highly recommend that expected givers be visited personally, your congregational culture will influence the way you choose to ask donors to give.

There is no harm in asking a donor for an amount that is beyond their perceived ability to give. The donor is always free to give what he or she chooses. If you ask for a minimal amount, that is often what you will get.

In large congregations it may be impossible to visit every potential giver. In such instances, the next best way of asking is by telephone. The least productive way, although used in almost all capital campaigns, is through the mail.

A capital campaign is not over until a closing celebration has been held. Donors to the capital campaign need to be individually thanked for their contributions and pledges. Beyond that, there is much to be gained by celebration for the entire congregation and other donors as well. A nice celebration meal is a time to give thanks and recognize the significance of the gifts that have been given. It is also a time to acknowledge God's blessings as manifested in this effort. And finally, it is a time to honor the contributions of the many volunteers who helped to make the campaign a success.

An excellent resource covering the details of a capital campaign is *With Generous Hearts* by Glenn N. and Barbara L. Holliman.[13] This book is not a "how to" for congregations to use in conducting their own capital campaign. Rather, its purpose is to acquaint readers with the details involved in a campaign.

Outside Fund Consultants

Since a well-run campaign is both important and complex, many congregations use an outside fund consultant. Such consultants assist congregations in identifying campaign themes, stating the case for giving, identifying potential donors, organizing and training volunteers, producing materials, conducting feasibility studies, and so forth. Different fund consultants offer different services and raise funds using different strategies. That is why it is important to put in writing what your congregation expects from the consultants you consider. Be aware that, even with an outside consultant, capital campaigns require many, many volunteers to help with the various facets of the campaign—publicity, asking for gifts, organization, celebration, and so forth.

Outside consultants aren't free. Their fee is typically based on the time they need to invest in the project. Time is typically impacted by the size of the congregation. The code of ethics of the Association of Fundraising Professionals[14] considers it unethical for fund consultants to charge a percentage of the dollars raised. Reputable fund consultants quote a flat fee for their services. A capital campaign can be made or broken based on the competency and compatibility of the fund consultant with your congregation. That is why unusual care must be taken in the selection process. Appendix B offers a resource to help congregations select a fundraising consultant.[15]

Another step in selecting a highly qualified fundraising consultant is to ask the consultants to give you congregational references. Ask for references from those whose campaign went well and those for whom the campaign, for whatever reason, was less successful. Contact these congregations and ask to speak with their capital campaign chairpersons. Most congregants, clergy and lay alike, are more than happy to share their experiences with others who are embarking on a campaign. Below are some suggested questions to ask the congregations to whom you talk.

- What process did you engage in to select the fundraising consultant you used?
- What made you choose the one you did?
- To what degree do you consider your capital campaign a success?
- For what were you raising funds?
- What was your fundraising goal and how much did you raise? What percentage of your pledges did you receive?
- What was the most satisfying experience of your capital campaign? The most difficult?
- How would you describe the relationship between the fundraising consultant and the planning team? Between the fundraising consultant and the congregation? Between the fundraising consultant and the clergy?
- What do you know now that you wish you would have known before your capital campaign began?
- What am I forgetting to ask that you think I should know?

Congregations, when interviewed about the most important factors contributing to the success of a capital campaign led by an outside fund consultant, name the following: having the congregation's commitment to the vision, focusing on spirituality as well as money, engaging the entire congregation, and making sure the consultant was a good fit with the congregation's theology and personality.[16]

Though many congregations use outside consultants, some congregations elect to conduct capital campaigns solely with volunteer leadership from within their congregation. The rationale is that an outside fundraiser is too costly. Volunteer leadership of a capital campaign can succeed provided steps similar to the ones expressed above are used—creating a case statement, designating the financial goal, identifying potential donors and their level of giving, asking for the gift, and celebrating success. To be successful, though, remember that a capital campaign needs to be highly organized. It calls for persistence and follow-up in soliciting the gifts of the congregation. And, like a campaign led by an external capital fundraising consultant, it calls for many volunteers from the congregation.

The authors of *The Complete Guide to Capital Campaigns for Historic Churches and Synagogues*[17] have provided the following checklist to help congregations assess whether they have the in-house skills to conduct their own capital campaign.

- Legal expertise: Ability to devise language for pledge cards and other documents.
- Writing ability: Skill to compose brochures, letters of request, press releases, etc.
- Fundraising experience: Not just for gift solicitations, but also for the organization and record-keeping systems of a campaign.
- Photographic and graphic design skills: Ability to design letterhead, brochures, invitations, etc.
- Research skills: Ability to research individuals, foundations, corporations, government sources, and genealogical records.
- Public relations expertise: Ability to place stories and attract other favorable publicity in both print and broadcast media.
- Leadership expertise: Experience in training volunteers and in group dynamics.

- Computer expertise: Experience to help choose hardware and software if you do not plan to use a manual gift-tracking system.

The Complete Guide authors recommend seeing if these skills exist within your congregation. If several of them are missing, you should hire an outside fund consultant.

If your congregation is undertaking multimillion-dollar projects in phases, it is usually the practice to engage in successive capital campaigns in a three-year cycle of pledges to the campaign. That means conducting a capital campaign every three years to ensure funding for multiple phases of the project. Sometimes a building project at a new location requires multiple capital campaigns. One may pay for the land, while another covers site development. The final phase is for the actual building. Congregations who know this in advance are better equipped to deal with a long process than congregations who assume that one capital campaign will enable them to achieve a new building.

Alternatives to Capital Campaigns

Some congregations find traditional capital campaigns unsuitable for their culture. This may be because the capital campaign giving pyramid does not "fit" them. Perhaps they cannot afford to hire a fund consultant. Maybe they don't have the capacity to have an internally led campaign. Experience has shown them that other strategies work better. As the Center for Congregations has worked with congregations, we have seen a variety of ways of raising money for building projects. In one congregation trying to raise two hundred thousand dollars to renovate an industrial building for a family life center, the pastor challenged each family to give one thousand dollars. While he acknowledged that some members could not afford that amount, the thousand-dollar challenge was established as a goal. Everyone was encouraged to give what she or he could. In addition to family giving, many groups in the congregation—women's group, youth group, men's group—came up with their own fundraising projects. The congregation met its financial goal.

We know of some congregations that encouraged their regular givers to increase giving by a certain percentage to raise the needed funds. For some congregations this is a simple but effective approach.

Another approach used in some Protestant congregations is often called "Miracle Sunday." This initiative is carefully planned for ten weeks leading up to a particular Sunday. On that Sunday, gifts, not pledges, are brought for the offering. The offering is taken early in the worship service. That way the total received can be announced. Successful Miracle Sundays require the building up of enthusiasm through congregational meetings, mailings, and worship. Potential major givers are visited, not to request a gift, but to ask what they are hearing and feeling about Miracle Sunday. Gifts from donors' current capital rather than pledges from future income are sought in a Miracle Sunday approach. This often includes noncash gifts, such as cars, bonds, real estate, stocks, jewelry, and so forth. Miracle Sunday offerings can bring in 50 to 150 percent of the annual income. Further information about Miracle Sundays is found in the *Abingdon Guide to Funding Ministry*.[18]

The Center for Congregations learned about another approach from a young, rapidly growing suburban congregation planning to relocate for more space. After having two successive capital campaigns for their relocation, the pastor realized that meeting the space needs of this growing congregation would require three-year capital campaigns as far into the future as he could see. He discerned that multiple successive capital campaigns emphasizing sacrificial giving was not an honest approach for this congregation. Instead, he chose to focus on the spiritual aspects of stewardship in general. Furthermore, he challenged the congregation not to move forward on its building project until their annual budget had risen sufficiently that they could afford mortgage payments for their building project(s). By building their space expenditures into the operating budget, they would be able to avoid further capital campaigns. The pastor reported an amazing increase in giving to the annual budget.

Determining how to raise money is a decision your congregation must make. To ponder your options, ask, "What have we done successfully in the past? What mistakes have been made in the past from which we can learn to do things differently?"

Summary for Your Team

- Facility projects are expensive and typically demand resources beyond a congregation's annual budget.
- Very rough estimates of construction costs can be determined using online estimators and square footage guidelines.
- Project costs are 30 to 50 percent more than construction costs.
- Congregations can determine how much they can afford by analyzing their assets; determining if they want to incur debt, and if so, how much they can borrow; and estimating the amount they can raise through their fundraising strategies.
- Capital campaigns consist of a case statement, a financial goal, the identification of donors, the invitation to give, the collection of pledges, and a celebration.
- Capital campaigns can be led by outside fund consultants or inside volunteers.

- Alternative ways congregations can raise money include group fundraisers, challenges for a certain amount, Miracle Sundays, budget increases, and so forth.

Questions for Your Team

1. When did your congregation last raise money for a project beyond your annual budget? What was the project? How were the funds raised? Was that fundraising effort success-ful? Why or why not?
2. Which of the fundraising strategies described appealed most to you as a team?
3. What unique aspects of your congregation need to be con-sidered when you select ways to raise funds?

PART 3
Do

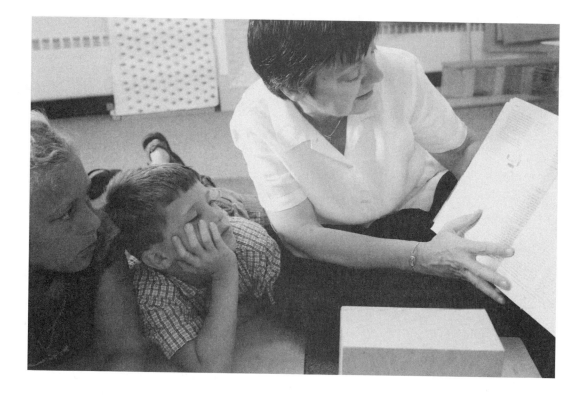

CHAPTER 8 How Will We Keep the
Congregation Informed?

Communication

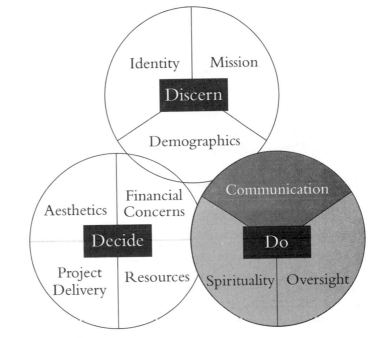

M any of us have played the popular game that goes by many
names—Telephone Operator, Pass It Down, Gossip, and more.
Participants form a circle. The first person thinks of a phrase and
whispers it as quietly as possible to his or her immediate neighbor.
The neighbor whispers the message to the next person. This continues
until the message reaches the last person, who says aloud what he or
she heard. The fun, of course, is that the message changes along the
way. "The moon is full" becomes "Phil's broom is cool." Keeping the
message clear is harder than it seems.

137

That is likewise true when communicating during a building project. And because there is more at stake than fun and games in a building program, you need to communicate as well as you can. Otherwise, the message "We're exploring refinishing the pews" becomes "We've hired a wrecking crew." Effective communication is essential at the beginning, middle, and end of every successful building project.

In the *do* phase of the sacred space model, addressed in chapters 8, 9, and 10, the questions you will explore will often begin with "how." Questions in this chapter include "How will you keep your congregation informed?" and "How will those responsible for the project communicate with the governing board?" Your congregation will find its own way to communicate based on your culture, your type of project, and your creativity.

For congregations, communication is about sharing information so that people can make good decisions and feel part of a project contributing to the common good. Good communication provides safe expression for strong emotions, demonstrates that leaders are using their power wisely, and creates a sense of community. Sharing information during a building program strengthens relationships, manages power, and creates a sense of cooperation on an important project.

Think of how stressful it is for a family to renovate its home. Knock out a wall and spouses snap at each other. The kids don't know where to play. Now multiply the stress of one household by the many households in a congregation and you see how building programs have the potential for bringing out less than the best behavior in your members. One way to lower the stress is to make sure people know what to expect. The best way to do this is to communicate frequently, accurately, and creatively during the building process. If you find yourself thinking, *Hmm, maybe we should let others know what is happening*, that's a good sign that you should make a phone call or write another message for the bulletin. Trust your best intuitions about whom to communicate with and when.

Communicate Frequently

You can't communicate too much. Group communication requires repetition, so plan on reporting important details at least five times. Many people won't hear what you say the first time, and those who do hear may need to hear several times before they fully understand what you are saying. Plan on spending a lot of time thinking about when and how to tell others what is happening. Spending time early on figuring out how to communicate about a project saves time you would spend later clarifying details and solving conflicts.

Communicate more frequently than you want to and provide more information than you think necessary. But realize that no matter how much you communicate about the sacred space project, there will still be people who say they didn't know that the new carpet would be green or that the nursery was being moved closer to the sanctuary. The goal of communication is to minimize this not knowing as much as possible even though you can't eliminate it entirely. The burden of communication is on the sacred space team or the governing board, not on the listeners.

Starting regular communication when the decision has been made to move ahead with a project is too late. Instead, it needs to begin in the initial planning stages and occur weekly during every phase (discern, decide, and do). Weekly communication must include both information already provided and new information. You will know you are communicating fully when people repeat back to you what you have communicated (e.g., "I heard that the plans will be in the gathering space for us to see this week"). If people are not giving you feedback, then you are not communicating frequently enough or with enough clarity. Silence from congregants is a signal that messages aren't being heard. When someone in the congregation asks a question that has not been considered or communicated, that question should be discussed by the team the next time it meets. The results of that discussion should be communicated back to the congregation and especially to the person who asked it.

Ways of Communicating

In addition to repetition, vary the ways you communicate. There are many different ways to tell what's happening regardless of where you are in the building process. Look early on for different ways to deliver your message. Which of the ones listed below will work for you?

- worship bulletins
- newsletters
- Web site
- bulletin boards
- face-to-face conversations
- building blogs
- annual reports
- dramas
- worship announcements
- e-mail
- DVD presentations
- Web cams
- thank-you notes

Building projects provide an opportunity not only to tell more about the building, but also to establish new patterns of communicating more about all aspects of congregational life. Other teams can be challenged to communicate as clearly and creatively as the sacred space team. Even during the building process, one congregation we know made sure that every printed announcement about the progress of the new roof was followed with a story about how mission dollars were being used. That is a great example of matching building news to ministry news and reinforcing that the whole point of building is supporting the congregation and its mission.

The way you communicate at the beginning of a project sets the tone for the whole effort. Healthy communication early on builds trust. Keep your messages as positive as possible without being disingenuous or inaccurate. A positive tone lowers anxiety and enforces the reality that obstacles can be overcome.

When your governing board decides to undertake a building project, it is helpful for your members to hear about that decision in the same way at the same time. If some members know about the project before or in a more personal way than other members do, some people will feel that the process is not fair and that their voices will not be heard. One pastor we know says that when the governing board voted to start a building feasibility study—after three months of discussion and discernment—he arranged for the building committee leader to announce it in worship the following Sunday. He also made it the lead article in the newsletter the next week. The message was too important to be communicated by word of mouth. It went through official channels, and everyone heard the same message at about the same time.

Some of what you communicate will be about the decision-making process before building begins. Some will be information sharing as the project progresses. Some will be about both decision making and the project's progression.

Invoking God

Clear communication during decision making is important. One leader remembers what happened as the congregation gathered to decide whether to build a new wing for education with a sparkling new kitchen or to wait three years and see if attendance continued to increase. Before people voted, the chairperson said, "We've prayed and prayed about this, and it is clear to us that to move ahead now to build the new wing is God's will. Please join us." The next day the pastor logged on to her computer and read an angry e-mail from a member. "How could the chairperson say it was God's will? Who decided?" These conversations are tricky. The fact is that what a leader says carries more weight than other voices. Words hold all kinds of spiritual and emotional freight. This is especially true while making a crucial decision. That's why it is important for a leader to be accurate about what is at stake when people vote. For some faith traditions, announcing God's vote ahead of time is manipulative. In others, it is a sign of vision and blessing. You need to prayerfully consider and even negotiate how to use faith language when talking about your building project.

Communicating Decisions

Decision-making communications include keeping members informed *before* they cast votes. It includes telling the congregation about options, scenarios, designs, budgets, and so on before decisions have to be made. Healthy decision-making processes involve clear messages between the governing board, the sacred space team, the building and grounds committee, and any others who have responsibility over the building. Share information generously before people have to make decisions. Sometimes sacred space teams are reluctant to share information because they worry it will stir conflict. But avoidance always adds to the conflict, because it makes the disagreement twofold: about both the content and the process of the decision. Frequent, clear, and creative communication about a building project keeps potential conflict focused on the building and not on processes, personalities, and power.

Your sacred space team must be strategic about when it shares specific information. For instance, a team may decide to withhold information when the information is unclear to them or when they need more data. You should withhold information only because you need more clarity and accuracy, never to change the outcome of a vote. Congregations make the best decisions about building projects when everyone has the same information. All voters should be clear on what they are being asked to decide well before the decision time.

It is vital that the governing board and sacred space team define a decision-making process and stick with it. At the outset of the project, clarify what kinds of decisions the team can make and what kinds of decisions need to be brought before the leadership of the congregation (or the entire congregation).

Likewise, keeping the congregation informed during the actual construction is essential. Routines changed by the messy presence of machinery and paint tarps are stressful. Some of that stress can be alleviated by letting parishioners know where the messy places will be each week.

In one congregation, the leader of the Interfaith Hospitality Network team took the elevator down to the basement. As was her usual routine, she planned to make sure the lights were on and the thermostat set at a comfortable temperature. She turned the corner and flipped the switch. The lights went on. What she saw was not what she expected. The kitchen wall had been torn out and the floor was covered with plaster. She took out her cell phone and called the chairperson of the sacred space team. "What happened?" she exclaimed. "We can't host twenty-five people tonight!" The gentleman on the other end of the phone said, "Oh, no one told you? They started on the basement this morning."

Congregations find it helpful to appoint a primary communicator, perhaps the chairperson of the sacred space team or a team member with special gifts in communication. All communications about the building process go through him or her to ensure that a consistent message is shaped and shared. This one person doesn't make all decisions about what is communicated and when. Others must be involved, especially the pastor and any others appointed by the governing board.

Clergy Involvement

So how involved should the clergy leader be? When we asked a group of fifty congregational leaders in the Indianapolis area this question, the answers varied. Some lay leaders stressed that a clergy person should not be the primary communicator. "It puts too much responsibility on them," one person said, "and makes people think that they care more about buildings than spirituality." Others said that the clergy leader should be the public face of the project because his or her words carry more weight, and that without clear communication from the clergy, no building project will succeed. "Pastor Jane is our leader," one person explained. "We want to know what she is thinking." Clergy participate in building projects in different ways.

Whatever shape that participation takes, congregants will want to know that their clergy leader cares and knows what is going on.

We have found that the extent to which clergy members are involved in communications is highly influenced by the congregation's culture. If the pastor is primarily seen as a shepherd or a priest, then it is often best for the clergy person to be actively engaged in the project but not overly visible. In this case, the pastor might write articles observing what's happening or affirming the leadership of others but not expressing the primary message. If the pastor is perceived primarily as a chief executive or a prophet, or if a congregation's governing system places power in the office of the clergy, then it makes sense for the clergy leader to take a central role in communication.

In *Building for Effective Mission*, Kennon Callahan describes the value of providing excellent pastoral care during a building program. Communication is one way of providing that care, because it keeps people settled and confident. Callahan encourages congregations to create or reenergize a shepherding team (deacon or care team) during the building project. More calls, more cards, more acts of kindness help put people at ease. It is important to steer conversations to life; don't fixate on the latest building news. Good communication involves conversation about much more than the building![1]

More Than Information

Barnes United Methodist Church in Indianapolis found that to be true. Barnes is an urban congregation. Their building project included renovating a kitchen for a weekly meal program and expanding their education space. They used numerous ways of keeping the congregation informed. Their sacred space team leader coordinated all communication. During the decision-making process, Barnes set up a network of small group discussions. During each major phase of the process, they sought feedback from every congregational group (even those without governing responsibility). Whether it was the ushers or the choirs, they were brought together for question and answer sessions. This way the groups within the church, governing or nongoverning, were kept up to date about what was happening at major decision points. Keeping the groups informed and engaged in a "relational" setting rather than only in a "governance" setting lowered anxiety and allowed important issues to be talked about without the pressure of an official vote.

Sometimes it is best to use small group gatherings as listening sessions and not information sessions. At different points your sacred space team will want to listen before it speaks or decides. At listening sessions it is more important for the team to do just that—sit and listen. If someone asks a simple, clear question, then offer a simple, clear answer. Remember, however, the main goal at listening sessions is to hear from others. Often, what happens at these listening sessions, particularly when they are healthy, is that people will tell stories about their own history with the congregation and the building. Recounting the past and being heard creates space for a congregation to move ahead with new building plans. Sharing stories honors and defuses the emotion behind them, thereby allowing a group to move forward.

As Barnes UMC moved from decision making to the building process, they designated a section of the weekly bulletin for the "building update of the week." The sacred space team leader or someone recruited by him spoke twice a month during worship. She or he provided an oral update, reinforcing the message in the bulletin and adding one or two more facts. These messages were short—less than two minutes—yet they provided helpful information, "Our pledges are almost there" or "The paint goes on this week," with a human face.

Why was this congregation so intentional about communication? Their team leader explained, "Our two biggest fears as a team were that people would feel that the team was making decisions without board approval and that we were spending money without letting the congregation know about it." So the team regularly printed budgets in the bulletin. They were also transparent about giving levels and expense disbursements.

Communicating Creatively

What worked well for Barnes United Methodist may or may not work well for your congregation. In any case, their story illustrates the importance of communicating frequently, accurately, and creatively in a way that makes sense for a congregation's culture, context, and preference.

Those considerations were also important to a Jewish congregation building at a new site. Many of their members were technologically savvy, so the building team set up an on-site live video camera. During the project, members could go online and watch what was happening in real time.

Another creative communication strategy was used by a small Baptist congregation that sent a letter to every household before any congregational meeting about the building program. The letter highlighted each motion and the rationale behind each recommendation.

Then there was a rural Presbyterian church that paid their architect to attend several gatherings. This ensured that the architect was part of a positive communication network. She was a good listener and she learned a lot about the congregation by eating with various groups. When it came time to approve the master plan, the vote was overwhelmingly positive. By that time the congregants felt close, not only to the plan, but also to the person who created it. Not all congregations can arrange or expect this from their architect. However, as you will read in chapter 10, congregations that communicate well with the professionals working on the endeavor find that they are much more satisfied with the overall project.

Keeping people informed during the project allows them to feel that they are part of the project. A creative way one congregation kept people informed was by inviting members to take hard-hat tours when interior work was going on. Another congregation started construction during the winter. Since many of their members lived in Florida during the winter, the congregation created an e-mail list of all their Florida members and sent them weekly progress reports. You'll want to think of informative, fun ways of keeping your congregation up to date.

The way you communicate during times of conflict surrounding the building project can help or hinder the progress. Defensive responses aggravate problems. That's why it is helpful to refer difficult questions or anxious people to your primary communication person. This person must remain calm and move closer to the person who is upset even if he or she doesn't agree with the complaint. For example, when the sacred space team receives a letter about the building project, it is incumbent upon the chief communicator to respond in writing. Otherwise, distrust festers and relationships become distant.

Remember that the past speaks. People recall things about previous building projects that did not go well, and these bad memories stir bad feelings in the present. You can learn a lot by listening to these stories. They are signals from the past to the present. They make leaders aware of possible problems to avoid in the present. Listening to these negative stories can also help the leaders devise a communications strategy that points out the differences between the past problems and the present project.

Coming up with just such a strategy is what a historic congregation at the edge of new urban development did. The congregation was looking to expand its sanctuary. After worship one day, members walked out to their cars and found flyers under their windshield wipers. The flyers were negative. They were also untrue. The leaders of the sacred space team knew who had distributed the flyers and knew that this group remembered a previous building program in which treasures were removed from the sanctuary without approval. People had been understandably upset about this. Since the leaders of the sacred space team were aware of these feelings, they knew they should react calmly to the flyers. They didn't respond by saying, "These people are against everything." Instead, they responded by saying, "These people were hurt before. We won't let what happened then happen again."

Good communication supports all aspects of a building project. Your facility is changing. That change also changes something in people. These changes, whether redoing the kitchen or moving to another site, shift people's experience of the holy and also change relationships. These changes are important, so listen to one another. Speak clearly. Repeat key messages. Sacred space is about building a community of God's people.

Summary for Your Team

- Healthy congregations communicate well. During a building program, you need to communicate better than well.
- Communicate more than you want to and more than you think you should.

- Communication is about more than letting people know facts. Sharing information during a building program strengthens relationships, manages power, and creates a sense of cooperation on an important project.
- Share a lot of information before people make decisions. People should be clear on what they are being asked to decide long before the time of decision.
- You know you are communicating enough when people repeat back to you what has already been communicated

Questions for Your Team

1. How will you make sure that you communicate better than well during the building process? Who will be responsible?
2. What role will the clergy leader take in communicating? Is this role consistent with the values of the clergy leader and the congregation?
3. How can you be creative? What creative forms can you use, at least occasionally, so that as you repeat the message, you still engage the listener?
4. How will you respond to negative comments? Will you talk about your plan so that you can be calm and consistent with your responses?

CHAPTER 9 How Will We Maintain
Our Spiritual Focus?

Spirituality

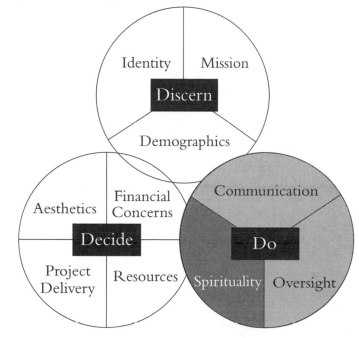

"**I** had too many volunteers for the building committee, so I had to move someone." That's how one pastor starts her story about moving a member from the building committee to the spirituality committee. "I chose the gentleman who was newest to the board. I didn't know any other fair way." The man made an appointment to talk with her. He walked in her study and said, "I do bricks. I don't do spirituality." Then he turned and left. At first the pastor didn't know what to do. For a week she thought and prayed. Then she made an appointment with the man. Soon he sat in her study. "Look, I'll put you back on the building committee," she said. "But you are now responsible for starting and ending each meeting with prayer!"

Bricks and prayer are not things we naturally put together. Bricks are solid, the stuff of the earth. And prayer is ethereal, the stuff of heaven. Nevertheless, bricks and prayer do go together. Spirituality and blueprints are both essential to a successful building program. Therefore, you need to make spiritual discernment a key component of spiritual life as you move through all phases of your building project. Your congregation's spiritual life is the mortar that keeps the bricks together. Building projects demand much—time, careful thinking, planning, generous giving, nuanced responses to conflict, and disruption of the everyday life of your congregation.

Focus on the spiritual dimensions of your life together so that the project's demands do not detract from your mission. The fact is that focusing on the spiritual life during a building project results in a double-strength effect. Your congregation becomes more vital as you learn how to experience holiness in the mundane *and* the sacred. Paying spiritual attention to that which seems everyday and ordinary (concrete, paint, hammers, and nails) makes it easier to see God at work in other aspects of life—work, home, play, and so on.

Spiritual Work

When we speak of spirituality, we mean the active consideration of what God is doing in your congregation through religious thought and disciplines true to your tradition. Spirituality, when linked to a building process, helps you think about how God is at work in the process of enhancing the place your congregation calls home. Participating in spiritual disciplines during the building process doesn't guarantee a perfect outcome. But it does make room for a closer relationship with God during this challenging time in your congregation's life.

The reason spirituality belongs to the *do* phase is because it involves activity—participation in practices that bring you closer to God and to your neighbor. It involves appreciating all phases of the building project as spiritual endeavors. Every aspect of the building project is loaded with spiritual meaning—the discernment process, the decisions about the building, and what goes on in the congregation during the construction phase.

This chapter introduces you to a variety of disciplines that will help the building process be an exercise in congregational spiritual development. Some of these suggestions will be a perfect match for your group. Others won't. We offer them to you, trusting that you will know best which will help you include God in your congregation's building project.

Working on a sacred space project is a spiritual process. Discernment and decision making require many conversations packed with discussion and debate. Conversations, even healthy ones, are not always smooth. They start and stop. Sometimes we speak with too many words and sometimes with too few. We get excited about an idea and interrupt our neighbor. We interrupt, not because we are rude, but because we are energized by ideas. Because conversations are not always smooth, paying attention to the spiritual aspects of the work is essential. And because the work is important, it calls for deeper attention to prayer than a mere rote petition to God at the beginning and end of meetings. Working with people having different ideas creates an opportunity for participants to experience the building process as a faith exercise. While attending to details of the building project, leaders must make sure that regular and new endeavors related to faith development occur in the congregation. Some may be things you are already doing; others may be new. The most effective sacred space projects are ones that (1) reinforce the spirituality of a group process, (2) recognize the spiritual nature of buildings, and (3) work toward the congregants' ongoing spiritual development.

People working on a building project are doing spiritual work. One way to live that reality is for a team to practice the spiritual disciplines that work best for them. For some it will be reading Scripture together; for others it will be spending time in silent prayer. Thankfully, our traditions offer many possibilities. For example, your team may find that scheduled moments of silent prayer help keep your attention on God and your mission. These silences need to be more than brief ten-second breaks. When a group takes regular time-outs for silence, it finds something holy. It is as if God takes a seat at the table. So, in addition to beginning and ending meetings with silent prayer, make sure there are silent breaks throughout the discussion. Such breaks help the group maintain its focus on the holy business of building.

Silence is just one spiritual exercise available to you. You need to discover your own way of attending to God during this process. We know one congregation that created their own ritual. They wanted a common prayer experience for their team and others in the congregation. Their team leader created a prayer card with a symbol of the church—a fleur-de-lis from their altar. On the backside of the card was a prayer written by the sacred space team that incorporated several passages of Scripture. The leader took the layout to the local print shop and had hundreds made. They gave them to all the members. The cards were distributed at each meeting about the building, whether it was a small group team meeting or a large group congregational meeting. The groups prayed their special prayer before and after each meeting. This attention to prayer helped the congregation focus on spiritual renewal as well as on the physical renewal of the building.

Consider Scripture

Another team, at the beginning of their first meeting, handed out copies of the *Good News Bible*. Why the *Good News Bible*? They were renovating the youth room, so they chose the same version of Scripture that the children and youth would use in their newly designed room. Beginning with that first meeting, the group read a chapter of Scripture before they attended to business. They started with the Gospel of Matthew and took turns reading sections. At the end of each chapter, the leader asked the group, "What did you hear that relates to our work?" This was not an exercise in scholarly exegesis; it was a way to juxtapose two holy things—Scripture and the work of the congregation—and see what new ideas emerged. In doing so, the Bible came alive to them in new ways.

That was especially evident at their fourth meeting when they read Matthew 4, where the devil tempts Jesus in the wilderness. One member said, "Remember how the devil placed Jesus on the top of temple. The devil said, 'You can fall and still be safe.' That's a lie." Another responded, "We are trying to create a special space. It might not save our kids from temptation, but it might contribute to helping them do what is right when the inevitable testing happens." This kind of interpretation, putting two unlike things together, creates holy sparks that shine new light on a subject. In this case, the two unlike subjects included a portion of Scripture and an aspect of their building program. The tension created by pairing such subjects provides the possibility of new meanings. In this case, the new idea was that a youth room is not so much a safe place, but a place where youth are taught how to creatively handle life's inevitable tests.

Another practice you might want to use during your sacred space project is the ancient prayer practice called *lectio divina*. Before a meeting, select a passage to study. You can choose a text from a weekly lectionary or a biblical text that seems interesting based on whatever the group is working on. *Lectio divina*, since it is a Latin phrase, may sound complex. Actually, it is easy to do and profound to experience. Begin by reading the passage. Read it twice, using two different readers. Then have the group reflect on the text silently. For a sacred project, have them think about how the text applies to their congregation, specifically to the building project. Next ask people to share their reflections, keeping in mind that the audience includes those present in the group and God, who is also present. Finally, end with a period of silence. That way God gets the last word. *Lectio divina*, like any spiritual exercise, does not automatically give you answers to your building questions, but it does include God in the conversation.

Receiving Help

Spiritual disciplines are simply a good idea. Faith communities have a number of times in their lives together when reading Scripture and praying together are good because they are part of the essential nature of a congregation. They are fundamental to being a people of God.

Even people of God find that building projects are difficult. One Presbyterian elder, working on a team deciding what to do with a ceiling that caved in, said, "We need all the help we can get!" Spiritual disciplines offer that help. And part of that help comes because practicing spiritual disciplines brings a group closer to God and to one another. Coming together is particularly helpful when a sacred space team is diverse or composed of people who don't know each other well. It is best the team not be a prefabricated in-group of like-minded people. As you can imagine, a diverse group of committed, gifted people will generate better ideas than a group in which everyone thinks alike. The categories of differences will vary from congregation to congregation. Sometimes the differences will be defined by age and sometimes by length of membership. Sometimes they will be identified by racial-ethnic background and sometimes by theological opinions.

Spiritual disciplines help people see and experience diversity as a strength. One project director we worked with looked at the strong and different personalities around the table and declared, "I can't do this. If it depends on me, it won't get done." She turned her worry into a prayer, one she shared with her team. Soon the group began its meetings with the same petition: "Lord, we're not doing this out of our need or our ideas, but the direction you want us to go." This prayer helped the group see their work as an ongoing conversation with God instead of a predetermined path they had to get right or else.

Since building projects stir deep emotions, a safe container for these strong emotions is needed. Thinking spiritually is a way of providing such a container. Spiritual disciplines can create a kind of security blanket in which to wrap the strong feelings stirred by building ideas.

Another thing spiritual disciplines can help with is to remind members that building projects are not a time for leaders to wonder, *Who among us is the greatest?* (see Luke 9:46). The work of a sacred space team is less about power and more of an upper room experience where each participant is taught to symbolically wash the feet of the other. Being spiritually focused leads team members to be mature in the way they handle differences and helps them to be willing to grow in this type of spiritual maturity.

People who participate in effective congregational building projects say that they often learn to listen better to ideas different from their own. One person who participated in a sacred space project said, "The Lord had to grow me up to see that my brothers and sisters don't think like me, don't act like me, and aren't going to do everything the way I would do it. I had to get more at ease at being uncomfortable. But it also built my confidence level and taught me how to love in spite of that."

Differences arise over all sorts of issues—big and small. And "big or small" depends on one's point of view. What is big for someone may seem small to another, such as when one person wants an elevator and another thinks a chairlift is just fine. Or someone advocates for a new youth room complete with video game stations, yet the teen who works on the project thinks that video games are a waste of time and doesn't think there should be a youth room at all. She thinks the youth should be meeting outside the church at Starbucks or the mall! If we learn to see these differences as uncomfortable nudgings from God, we can learn to work well with others without becoming offended and upset. Such a point of view teaches us the spiritual discipline of sitting still and listening to people whom God loves and who happen to have ideas different from ours.

Disagreements will arise—that's common for building projects. Often they are just bringing to light differences that have existed all along but have surfaced because of the stress of the building project. A congregation that uses spiritual disciplines and draws on the best of its faith tradition in terms of relationships and process will find that uncomfortable moments become more manageable and fewer. That is because practicing spiritual disciplines helps a team connect with God. When they do, they can deal more faithfully with their differences.

Spiritual Discernment

So how can spirituality support faithful decision making? It begins with clarity. The leaders of the congregation need to be clear about who makes what decisions regarding a building project. But this question of "who" is different than the question of "how." How a group makes decisions is a clear expression of their faith. Some processes are more positive than others. Your congregation may use Robert's Rules of Order in decision making. Robert's Rules are designed to make sure that all voices are heard in an orderly manner. However, building issues are rarely orderly; they are complex and messy. And so are discussions about them. Following Robert's Rules too slavishly can restrict discussion and restrain creativity. Conversations about whether to expand at your present site or move to a new location will go in a lot of directions until a group is ready to decide. Robert's Rules allows a group to discuss such issues only after a motion is made. This might work after details are hashed out but probably won't when the group is trying to get a handle on the direction it is trying to decide to go. Nobody is ready for a motion "to move across town"—or ready to be on record as the one making it.

Therefore, you will want to consider other forms of decision making. There are interactive means of decision making, many of them associated with historic spiritual practices. A resource you might find helpful is *Discerning God's Will Together* by Danny Morris and Charles Olsen. They describe in detail a ten-step decision-making process that draws on a variety of spiritual practices they call "stepping stones."[1] Below is a list of the ten stepping stones:

1. Framing—identifying the focus
2. Grounding—identifying values and boundaries

3. Shedding—laying aside preconceived notions
4. Rooting—connecting to a faith tradition
5. Listening—hearing the variety of opinions
6. Exploring—unpacking different options
7. Improving—making ideas the best they can be
8. Weighing—sorting and testing the options
9. Closing—bringing explorations to conclusion
10. Resting—testing the decision by letting it rest near the
    heart

When a sacred space team arrives at a crossroad, it can use this
process to avoid getting stuck.

Further Spiritual Activities

Spiritual activities, like faith, can be paradoxical. For example,
that which is absent can communicate the presence of God. At a
medium-sized mainline congregation that felt its congregation was
more diverse than it appeared, the chairperson of the sacred space
team placed an empty chair at the table at every meeting. He called
it the Elijah chair. He did so to honor the Jewish Passover tradition
in which an empty chair is placed at the family table in expectation
of Elijah's arrival. Whenever the team was stuck, or whenever the
leader sensed the group was at a crucial decision point, he asked
people to imagine someone whose voice hadn't yet been heard. They
took turns describing who was sitting in Elijah's chair and what that
person had to say to the group. This discipline helped them get beyond their own thoughts. Their ideas grew. The space became more
than a room—it was also a container for the Spirit.

Reading, silence, and a spiritual decision-making process may seem a bit abstract. Some groups need to see something concrete in order to attend to God. Sometimes it helps for a team to see their building through spiritual eyes. That was true for one group working on changing their sanctuary. That congregation asked a member to create three-dimensional models of the sanctuary as it used to be, as it was at present, and as it would look when they finished the process. When the group gathered for a meeting, they spent a few minutes looking at one of the models as if it were an icon and shared their memories or hopes. It helped their team to learn to see their building through spiritual eyes.

Another team took photos of their building. At each meeting's closing, they projected the photos on screen and formed prayers based on what they saw.

These examples show that just because this is a building project doesn't mean that it is too focused on material things to bring God into the conversation. If anything, the meaning of buildings—such as the ways they represent shelter and home—make paying attention to the spiritual aspects of bricks and mortar crucial.

Besides bricks, wood, and plaster, time also teaches us about God. That's especially true in building projects. Congregations find that building projects take longer than expected. The good news is that there is a spiritual element to waiting. You can choose to see delays as an unfair hardship or as invitations to live into God's timing. Sometimes it is hard to see things that seem to take too long in a positive light. However, most faith traditions have language and experience for reframing such delays as part of God's timing.

Building projects are advent time for congregations. They involve a lot of preparation. Before you can think about fundraising, you need to see the architect's plans. Or the carpenters call and say they cannot get to your project until next month. Like the liturgical season of Advent, you must wait, listen, and watch during a building project. You need to be ready for (and not done in by) surprises. Building projects are like what the four weeks of Advent are like for most Christian kids—is Christmas ever going to get here?

In Judaism the Hebrew month preceding the High Holy Days—Elul—is a time of preparation. You are getting ready to be penitent. To do that, the liturgy changes. You make penitential prayers, along with a request to be remembered in the Book of Life for another year. And you are supposed to be making reparations to people you have harmed. You are preparing to *build* your life for another year. Certain seasons of a building project can, like Elul, be a time for preparation before carpenters hammer nails and painters apply the paint.

Waiting has practical value too. During the time it takes for projects to unfold, the seemingly impossible becomes possible. Answers appear for difficult questions. Better alternatives emerge.

That is what a certain congregation wanting to add more rooms to their education wing found. The addition meant moving an office, putting up new walls, and cutting down a tree. The sacred space team told the governing board that the tree needed to be taken down. The leader of the governing board remembered that the tree had been a memorial gift and had grown next to the building for thirty years. The family who gave the tree hoped that it would grow for another thirty. So the governing board waited and made no decision. Some members thought the delay showed a lack of vision. Others agreed that it was best not to ruffle feathers.

Then the tree made its own decision: it died. The project went ahead—naturally.

Making decisions about building projects is spiritual work. Spiritual disciplines make the waiting and the working not only more manageable, but also more engaged with God.

Involve Your Congregation

Of course, spiritual attention during the building process shouldn't be limited to the sacred space team. Our sacred space program found that it was healthy for the entire congregation to focus on spiritual practices during a building project. We recommend that on the day your congregation announces the new project, it also starts a spiritual growth program. Here are some possible choices for your consideration:

- the *Renovaré* program, which introduces people to six different models of spiritual development
- *Companions in Christ*, a small group resource that is continually under development, with new studies constantly being added
- the Purpose Driven series by Rick Warren, which encourages people to find God-given direction for living
- Keeping Faith First, a whole community catechesis program that is a vision of faith formation rooted in the documents of Vatican II[2]

We are familiar with one congregation that challenged members to read the entire Bible. They started this spiritual project on the same day they voted to move to a new location. Another congregation redesigned their sanctuary to make it more accessible. During their building project, they began a prayer vigil ministry in the sanctuary. One day a week they opened their sanctuary doors and had at least one person present praying for the world and for the neighborhood. They lifted petitions to God while the workers lifted beams to support the new structures.

Remember the Lutheran church mentioned in chapter 3 that integrated discernment about their building plans and their everyday life of faith during Lent? They used their mission statement as a study guide. Each week during Lent, small groups met to talk about elements of their mission statement. Eighty percent of the congregation participated in at least one of the sessions.

Congregations find that opportunities for spiritual development keep their focus on God. And combining a spiritual growth program with a building program lessens the possibility that some members might think the clergyperson is taking too much time with the building and not enough for ministry.

Effective building projects do more than erect a facility or remodel space. They reinforce the spirituality of a group process and contribute to the ongoing spiritual development of congregants. Effective building projects also teach the congregation about the spiritual nature of buildings. We cannot overstress the truth that the material and the spiritual are not two separate realities. Shelter is sacred. Gathering space for the people of God directs people to God. Some of us are cynical toward buildings. We talk about how the money that goes toward building could be used for worthier projects, or we opine that buildings reflect a pastor's inflated ego. At times, these less than redemptive views of buildings are true. But more often than not, buildings communicate the stories of faithful people. A sacred space team needs to look for teachable moments during the building program that show the congregation the spiritual voice of its building.

The Spiritual Meaning of Buildings

A good way to do that is to think of the spiritual meanings of congregational buildings and then share these meanings. For some, particular places are holy because they are associated with specific events. A couple remembers they were married in the sanctuary. The youth room is the place where she met her best friend. The basement is where he ladled up the bean soup for the feeding ministry. Buildings are filled with sacred memories. You need to find ways of telling these stories not only during the building project, but at many different times in your life together.

For some traditions, place is an instrument that helps God fulfill God's mission. The building provides the means to God's good aims. For other traditions, the congregation's building is a reminder that all places are potentially holy. If no place is set aside as special, then no places are seen as special. If at least one place is set aside, then it helps us see other places as shelters for the spirit. Yet other traditions maintain that the place is not holy, but the meeting that takes place there is sacred.

By understanding your congregation's culture and theology, your sacred space team can help your entire congregation see how your buildings and grounds contribute to your understanding of God's story.

Particular Desires

Jon Pahl, a Lutheran theologian, asserts that sacred spaces exist to orient people to particular desires that support particular practices. In his book *Shopping Malls and Other Sacred Places*, he talks about three particular places: shopping malls, Disney World, and the suburban home. He addresses the way these places represent, and even create, particular desires. For instance, the shopping mall makes us want to buy. It does this through bombarding the senses and using floor plans that disorient us. That explains why it is so easy to get lost in a shopping mall.[3]

Buildings orient us to particular desires by using one of three general stances. Your building can reinforce desire. For example, a small circular sanctuary painted in soft colors accommodates a desire for intimacy with God. Or, conversely, your building can communicate resistance to a particular unwelcome desire. For example, a gathering space just outside the sanctuary that displays a row of flags from various countries—symbolizing the universal nature of baptism—resists the negative desire for a patriotism that puts down other nations. Your building might redirect a desire. An example of this would be an urban congregation between two office buildings that clears its small front lawn once a month to host a free farmers' market.

You can see this orientation yourself. Choose a part of your sacred space, the sanctuary or the youth room, for instance. What desire does this space stir? What longing do you want people to get a sense of when they walk though that sacred space? Is it a desire for prayer? Or maybe a desire for connection or generosity? Ask if the desire you want to achieve is the desire you feel the space supports. Or does the mood created by the space run contrary to its purpose?

Scripture uses metaphors for other desires our buildings create. Pahl names six New Testament metaphors that reorient us toward God's presence among us. These metaphors are living water, light of the world, rock of salvation, true vine, one body, and the city of God.[4] Think about how your space is an expression of one of these metaphors or another biblical metaphor that represents your faith community. Now think of ways it *could* be.

While talking to a group of congregation leaders, Pahl tells of taking his students to churches in Chicago. He wanted them to see how these congregations used light in very different ways to communicate God's activity and human desire. A Presbyterian church used light to reflect upon the depravity of humans, unconditional election, and limited atonement. A building built by the Irish used themes from the *Book of Kells* represented in earth tones of green and golds. Then Pahl describes a visit to Chicago's St. Olaf's Ukranian Catholic Church:

> You walk into the narthex and there are wooden doors keeping you from entering the sacred space. But then, the doors are opened and this is what you see: the icons. At the top is Jesus blessing the people and then down to the evangelists, the teachers, and farther down to the members of the congregation who built it. All of them represented in icons in the building. That is the understanding of salvation in the eastern tradition. In the western tradition, it tends to be sacrificial atonement. In the east, salvation is participation. Taking part with God. At its extreme, God became a person so that a person can become God. A dangerous notion and yet it is communicated in the place itself, woven into the community, the fabric, the beauty and warmth and color and vibrancy and light. . . . Light, the light of the world. We don't wake up in the morning if that sun doesn't come up.[5]

There are several reasons for attending to spiritual things during a building program. First, your sacred space team's participation in spiritual practices—prayer, Scripture reading, and other practices appropriate to your faith community—include God as a participant in the process. This is its own good. It is never a *bad* idea to practice group prayer and Scripture study. Prayer and Scripture reading create their own good, regardless of whether they are "useful" or not.

Another reason to attend to spiritual things during a building program is to encourage the entire congregation to get closer to God. In our experience, sacred space teams report that their decision making is wonderfully improved when spiritual disciplines become a regular part of their time together. Spiritual disciplines support all the active phases of your project.

Moreover, a building project is the right time to start a spiritual project, because the two will intersect at natural points. God's place in the building will be more apparent, and the building's connection to spiritual growth will be more strongly constructed.

Some people say that places are sacred because God made them that way, such as Jerusalem or the site of a particular miracle. Other people say that human beings construct sacred places because of the meaning we attach to them, like a community's one-hundred-year-old prairie church building or your grandparents' home. The reality is somewhere in between. God's Spirit has its own way. And we have the ability to make our own meaning. Paying attention to the things of God makes a building program into a *sacred* space project.

Summary for Your Team

- Make spiritual discernment a key component as you move through all phases of your building project. Your congregation's spiritual life serves as the mortar that holds the bricks together.
- Building projects take longer than congregations expect. Building projects are an advent time. Prepare for them through prayer, Scripture reading, and other disciplines that fit your faith community.
- Congregational buildings hold spiritual meaning. The building is the means to God's good aims. Your sacred space team can help the entire congregation see how their buildings and grounds contribute to God's story.
- Building projects are demanding. Your faith is sustained through spiritual disciplines. Making decisions about building projects is spiritual work.

Questions for Your Team

1. What spiritual disciplines fit your team the best? Who will be responsible for leading them?

2. What process are you going to use to make decisions about your building project? How will you add a spiritual dimension to the process?

3. How will you include the entire congregation in disciplines of spiritual growth during the building project?

4. What human longing do you associate with your facility? Is this longing something you want to accommodate, resist, or reframe?

5. Name a Scripture image that you associate with your building. How will your new building, addition, or renovation express images from Scripture?

CHAPTER 10 How Will We Ensure That the Work Is Done Properly?

Oversight

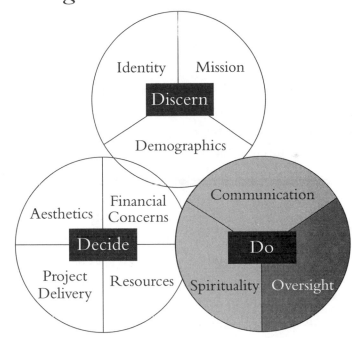

*A*downtown congregation with dwindling membership and a building far too large for its needs and its maintenance capacity discovered that it needed a new roof. They interviewed four roofing companies. The one with the most reasonable cost was selected to do the work. In less than six months, they counted twenty-five leaks. Frustrated, they contacted the roofing company only to discover the phone number was disconnected. The roofer had gone out of business. They then contacted another company who had bid but not been chosen. That roofer told them, "I knew this would happen. Each day

173

I sat and ate my lunch where I could see the roofers. I could have told you that it was not being installed correctly."

Another congregation that contacted the Center for Congregations for resources on guttering firms noted that they had roofing and moisture problems that needed to be resolved. As we often do, we asked whether the congregation had ever considered conducting a conditions assessment.[1] Such a facility assessment is a thorough inspection by an architectural firm or other facility experts, such as a commercial inspector, structural or civil engineer, or other skilled professional. The expert fully examines the facilities to determine their condition and to see if any repairs need to be made. The facility committee of the congregation decided this would be a good idea and hired an inspector. As a result, the congregation learned that the builders of their ten-year-old education wing had taken many shortcuts. Water had been leaking behind the building's exterior, and the leakage had rotted the wooden frame. Fixing the problem meant removing and replacing the complete facade.

Unfortunately, these congregations' costly difficulties are replicated in various ways by many congregations. When congregations fail to ensure that what the contractors do is what the congregation hired them to do and that the work is done in a quality manner, there are often costly mistakes.

So can your congregation avoid experiences like these? How can you ensure that the work is being done properly? We will explore these questions in this chapter on oversight, the final aspect of the *do* phase of the sacred space model.

Theological principles underscore the need for a congregation to build with sufficient oversight to ensure the highest possible quality. The most obvious principle, no matter what one's faith tradition, is stewardship of time, money, and energy. An investment in oversight of the work inevitably saves additional expenses and avoids shoddy work.

Just as unnecessary expense is often incurred when a building project goes over cost or requires costly fixes, so the time and energy of a congregation is drained away from other ministries when building problems emerge after a building project is completed. Remember the earlier account of the dwindling congregation that pooled their resources to reroof their building only to discover the work had not been done properly, and they needed to pay even more to remedy the problem? This discovery not only affected them financially but also discouraged their spirit. It required investing significant time and energy as they tried to figure out what to do next.

In the same way that a congregation's building is an expression of its mission, so, too, is the building process an expression of the congregation's values and identity. If no arrangement is made for congregational oversight of your building project, you not only run the risk of wasting time, money, and energy, but also of having an end product that is, at least in some respects, less than you expected. So, how can you ensure that the work is being done properly?

An Advocate

The first step in avoiding a bad experience is recognizing that building projects involving new construction and/or major expansion or renovation/restoration require that an advocate for the congregation oversee the process. What we mean here by "oversee" is to check regularly on the building process. We don't mean direct the project. That is the responsibility of the architect and builder. The advocate for the congregation knows the needs, interests, and desires of the congregation and monitors the entire process to ensure that those needs and interests are met. Later in the chapter we will discuss the possibilities for filling this advocacy role.

Congregations want to ensure that the work they contract for is done on time. Often this requires persistence and timely monitoring of the vendors performing different aspects of the work. Part of one congregation's sanctuary remodeling was having their pews removed and refinished. They vacated their sanctuary during the remodeling and planned to hold their Easter service in the remodeled sanctuary. The pew refinishing, scheduled with plenty of time and promises from the company that they would be reinstalled in time for the Easter service, kept being delayed. It took a representative from the congregation some persistent and persuasive contacts to ensure that the company did deliver the pews on time. The congregation's proactive approach ensured that they had what they needed when they needed it.

Making sure that the work is done properly also includes monitoring the budget. All building projects require some funds be designated for contingencies. However, allowing unrestrained cost overruns is not responsible stewardship. One congregation in the Indianapolis area undertook a significant building expansion. They decided to save forty thousand dollars by not hiring an owner's representative. During the project, things went awry. They ended up with a hundred-thousand-dollar overrun on drywall alone. In hindsight, they acknowledged not having an owner's representative was a costly mistake.

It goes almost without saying that congregations need to monitor the quality of the work being done. This does not mean an inspection by the building committee when it is time to create the final punch list. Rather, it means an ongoing observation and inspection throughout the entire process. Is insulation being installed where needed? Is the lumber used split or warped? Are protections made when pouring concrete in the winter? Is the carpet the right color and laid where the plans call for it to be? It is impossible to predict the kinds of things that need to be examined. Only a regular routine inspection by a representative for the congregation will be able to spot the kinds of quality-related issues that inevitably emerge.

Another way to ensure that your work is being done the way you desire is to manage appropriately requested changes, commonly called "change orders," and their costs. In a building project, issues inevitably emerge that were unanticipated by the architect, design-build firm, contractor, or congregation. For example, a congregation working on a new building or expansion may discover midway through the project that they need more storage space than their original design allowed. If this is discovered early enough in the project, adjustments can be made. However, such changes mean additional expense. A congregation, typically through its designated advocate, communicates the desired change to the architect or contractor and negotiates and documents a fair price. Change orders and resulting costs must be managed so that necessary and affordable changes can be implemented and "project creep"—numerous things added to the project as it progresses, resulting in growing costs and extended time frames—is avoided.

In addition to change orders addressing unexpected changes in the building phase, many other kinds of unexpected dilemmas confront congregations during building projects—things such as a nearby new development improperly installing a drainage system, causing water to flow onto your property and impacting your building plans; or being told when you apply for a permit that your parking lot is located in an easement and you need to prove when your parking lot was added; or your request for variance not being approved because neighbors don't want more traffic in their neighborhood. The list goes on and on. Congregations who want to ensure that their building project is being done properly will need patience to deal with these unexpected delays. Furthermore, they will want to act with integrity while advocating for the needs of the congregation.

Chapter 8 focused primarily on communication within the congregation, but it is also important to work on communication between the congregation and the architect and builder. Repeated communications—requests for information, probing questions, appropriate listening, and statement and restatement of things that may seem obvious—are crucial to the quality of both the process and the end result. Contractors must sometimes make on-the-spot design interpretations without being able to confer with the congregational representative. And sometimes these decisions result in judgments that may not fit the needs of the congregation. The only way to ensure that your needs are met is to communicate, repeatedly, your needs to the builders.

One congregation remodeling their education wing discovered that the only door to one of their classrooms led into another classroom instead of into the hall. The contractor had put it there in spite of plans. For the congregation, however, entering the remodeled classroom only from the classroom next door was an impractical and unacceptable solution. They communicated their needs clearly to the contractor, who rectified the situation.

When we ask, "How will we ensure that the work is done properly?" we mean not only the final project, but also the process employed to achieve it. One of the challenges of the process is that building projects often generate at least some conflict. Differences of opinion among the designer, builder, and congregation are inevitable, as the above illustration shows. The goal is to resolve these differences in respectful, satisfactory ways.

We have reviewed a number of ways that congregations can ensure that their building project is done properly. These include having an advocate; closely monitoring the time schedule, delivery, and quality; managing change orders; dealing with unexpected issues; communicating actively and persistently; and resolving conflict appropriately. We now turn to the question of who can help a congregation make certain that these issues are addressed. Options include a congregational volunteer, a congregational staff member (not the pastor), a paid owner's representative, and/or a building inspector.

Owner's Representative

People performing oversight duties for building projects are often referred to as owner's representatives. The owner, in this case the congregation, of the facility being built, renovated, or restored, hires or designates the owner's representative. If hired, the representative is paid for his or her work. If designated, he or she is a volunteer (although, as you will read below, it is important to have contractual or covenantal arrangements regardless). The owner's representative, whether paid or volunteer, addresses the issues above and ensures that the project is completed with the highest of standards.

As we said in the earlier chapter on resources, selecting the best vendors has a major impact on your satisfaction with the finished product. Using the best architects and builders should result in work that is as good as possible. So why is an owner's representative necessary? An owner's representative monitors inevitable glitches and ensures that they are resolved to your satisfaction. At times an architect and contractor may think the work is completed, but the congregation's sacred space team sees that something has not been completed to the expected quality. Using an owner's representative provides a way of identifying and resolving these circumstances.

For smaller projects, having a volunteer from the congregation serve as the owner's representative often works well. However, if the volunteer is not a building professional, he or she may not be able to delve as deeply into the dynamics of the project as a trained professional might. Your congregation may have a member who is an architect or construction manager or who works in other facets of construction and is willing to volunteer as the congregation's owner's representative. The primary challenge to this is evaluating honestly with him or her whether or not he or she has the time to invest in this demanding role. We know of one new congregation constructing their first building that selected a member to oversee its project. The work was so demanding that the member, who owned his own consulting firm, took a leave of absence from his work to oversee the building. Although this may not be realistic for most people, it was a choice this person gladly made. At the open house for the new facility, he acknowledged that it had been a lot of hard work. But he also beamed with pride over the facility they had built and what it meant for their ongoing ministry. As the project concluded, he considered whether he would return to his job or whether God was prompting him to volunteer in other areas.

In another congregation, two retired men consider it their gift to the church to work at improving the facility so it is more attractive and welcoming for members and visitors. This work is their passion. They spend most days at their place of worship identifying what needs to be done and doing much of the work themselves. When their congregation embarked on a sanctuary remodeling project, these men were there daily. They monitored the work and ensured that a quality job was done.

Larger congregations often have a facility manager or administrator on staff. These staff members, because of their familiarity with the congregation and their facilities, make good owner's representatives provided some of their regular work can be delegated.

While facility or administrative staff members make good congregational owner's representatives, the pastor should never be the person designated to oversee a building project. When congregations fail to appoint an owner's representative, the pastor becomes the de facto owner's representative simply because he or she is on site more than anyone. Clergy persons have told us how they reached, or nearly reached, complete burnout as a result of doing their regular pastoral duties while overseeing a building project.

Pastors need to avoid the role of owner's representative because they have a key role in modeling a focus on shepherding throughout the building project. Congregational consultant Kennon Callahan states it this way:

> One mistake pastors sometimes make during a building project is to become involved almost as a second architect or contractor. When this happens, they neglect their role as a shepherd. The same is true with some of the congregation's gifted, shepherding leaders. They become caught up in the details of working drawings for the building and leave their shepherding less well tended.
>
> It is precisely during a building project that the shepherding by the pastor and gifted leaders is crucial. When you embark on a building project, pay particular attention to the congregation's needs for care.[2]

A congregations can avoid the unintended consequence of the pastor necessarily assuming the role of overseeing the building project by intentionally selecting or hiring an owner's representative. This brings us to consideration of a paid owner's representative for congregations whose project is bigger than can adequately be handled by a volunteer, who lack a willing volunteer, or who for other reasons deem it important to hire someone to fulfill this role.

In cases in which a construction manager is hired as a part of the building team (see chapter 5 on project delivery), he or she assumes the role of the owner's representative. In other cases, professional owner's representatives may have backgrounds as architects, construction managers, or engineers or may have other experience and training related to building. Many architectural firms offer owner's representative services. It is important to understand the distinction between the architect's role in the building process and that of an owner's representative. An architect's work is not over when a congregation approves a design. An architect is often involved with the congregation in selecting a contractor. Also, an architect oversees construction, making certain that her or his architectural plan is being implemented according to the design.

What makes the role of a paid owner's representative so valuable is that he or she works solely for the owner, in this case the congregation. As such, he or she does not have the interests of the architectural firm, the design-build firm, the contractor, or any other party hired for the building project as his or her main interest. The owner's representative is selected to make certain that the needs of the congregation are met. That is all.

An owner's representative may be involved at one of several levels. What your congregation needs depends on the size of your project, the capacity of your members, and the culture and practices of your community of faith. Multimillion-dollar building projects benefit especially from hiring a professional owner's representative. This person works with the congregation through the entire process from design to completion. In this scenario, the owner's representative ensures that the desires and needs of the congregation are met when the building is being designed, as well as when it is being built.

While in some instances an owner's representative participates in the design as well as the construction phase, in other cases the owner's representative begins working for the congregation during the actual building phase. In this case, his or her role is to ensure quality workmanship and make certain that the project remains on schedule and within budget.

Skills of an Owner's Representative

Certain qualifications, including skills, training, and personality attributes, make for an effective owner's representative. The National Society of Professional Engineers notes that an owner's representative needs to be "a keen observer, a tactful communicator, knowledgeable of the provisions of the contract documents, and a responsible and ethical person." Furthermore, he or she must have "a clear understanding of [the congregation's] policies, procedures, and culture."[3]

The United States Department of Energy adds that an owner's representative needs "sufficient authority to carry out responsibilities without ambiguity or interference; decisiveness—the ability to take necessary steps to get decisions made in a timely manner." The owner's representative cannot be one who procrastinates or second-guesses after decisions have been made.[4]

An owner's representative needs sufficient construction knowledge to be able to spot when something is not right and needs to be able to read and interpret blueprints and know how builders translate those plans. For example, if a blueprint calls for restrooms for the disabled, the owner's representative needs to be able to confirm that they are located according to the design and that the doors are wide enough for a wheelchair.

Equally important as the building skills and training is the owner's representative's ability to communicate well. As mentioned earlier in this chapter, a significant factor in the success of a building project is good communication between the congregation and building professional. When the owner's representative is a volunteer or staff member of the congregation, he or she is also the designated communicator with the builders. However, when an owner's representative is hired from outside of the congregation, he or she needs to communicate with the appointed congregational contact person. In such cases, the owner's representative needs the ability to suspend personal preferences and listen intently to the desires of the congregation for which he or she is working. This requires getting to know the congregation and building a trusting relationship. Similarly, a trusting relationship must be built with the design firm and the builders. Negotiating the desires and needs of the congregation is problematic if it is done in a caustic, demanding, or domineering manner. Rather, the representative needs to be firm, clear, and respectful.

Architects, construction managers, and gifted volunteers are options congregations can explore for owner's representatives. The goal is to find a responsible representative who ensures that the building project is well done.

When selecting an owner's representative, whether paid professional or volunteer, it is wise to interview several candidates. Questions to ask a prospective owner's representative are noted below. Not all, however, are appropriate for a volunteer.

- What experience have you had in architectural construction and/or historical renovation? (Your congregation can replace these terms with those more consistent with the work you need done.)

- What training and experience do you bring to your role as an owner's representative?
- In what ways does that training and experience equip you to do the work we are asking you to do?
- What do you see as key roles of an owner's representative? What can you do for us that a lay volunteer would not be able to do?
- For what kinds of organizations/buildings have you served as an owner's representative?
- How do you maintain consistent, clear communication with the congregation you are working with?
- Give us an example or two of how your services impacted the bottom line and/or the finished product for an organization you served.
- How do you negotiate the resolution of conflict between the congregation and the architect or builder?

You will also want to ask paid professionals to see a sample contract they sign with their clients and request at least three references, preferably congregations.

When hiring a person to serve as your owner's representative, you will want to have a signed contract delineating what you expect that person to do for the congregation. It needs to include at least the following information:

1. Duration of the agreement (e.g., from beginning of the design phase through the final occupancy or from the beginning of construction through final occupancy).
2. The tasks the owner's representative is expected to perform. These include visiting the site as often as specified;

maintaining a log with dates, decisions, conversations, and timelines; writing progress reports to the congregation; preparing and supervising punch lists; and so forth.
3. The name of the congregational contact person.
4. The compensation agreed upon.

You may find that an owner's representative has written contracts detailing the terms of the agreement. You need to make certain that all important areas are included in such a contract. Even when your owner's representative is a volunteer or congregational staff person, a written covenant describing numbers 1 and 2 above is advisable.

Commercial Inspectors

Besides owner's representatives, volunteer or hired, there is yet another professional who can aid congregations in ensuring that quality work is done—a commercial inspector. Many of us are familiar with hiring a home inspector to inspect a house before it is purchased in order to determine its condition and necessary repairs. Owners building a new house use home inspectors at various phases to ensure that everything is being done properly. An inspector gives the owner a written report of any substandard work that he or she discovers. Some, but not all, home inspectors also inspect houses of worship. Commercial inspectors focus on inspecting businesses, industry, and not-for-profits' buildings.[5] If there aren't any commercial inspectors in your area, ask home inspectors whether they are willing to inspect a place of worship. Home inspectors are not always able or willing to inspect steep roofs and other unique aspects of churches and synagogues, but some are.

An inspector, even one conducting a thorough inspection several times throughout the building project, is not as effective as having an owner's representative, volunteer or paid, on site on a regular basis. An inspector would have been helpful for the congregation described earlier that got a shoddy roof. The inspector could have warned the congregation what was done wrong, what the consequences would be, and how the problem could be corrected. On the other hand, a congregation would need an owner's representative to identify a potential budget overrun.

In summary, all congregations engaging in significant building projects need to intentionally arrange for a designated person to ensure the quality, budget, and schedule of the project. Some congregations may think that it is not necessary to have an owner's representative, whether volunteer or paid. Congregations that neglect this aspect of their building project, though, are often disappointed. Congregations that intentionally address their need for an advocate who monitors the project benefit by experiencing smoother management of the inevitable snags of a building project and enhancing the quality of the results.

Summary for Your Team

- Congregational building or renovation projects require oversight by someone whose sole commitment is to the needs of the congregation. This person is often called an owner's representative.
- Owner's representative is a role that can be assumed by a hired professional, congregational staff, or volunteers.
- Congregations that select an owner's representative avoid the unintentional result that the pastor may become the de facto owner's representative.

- Skills of an owner's representative include knowledge of construction, communication and negotiation skills, and decisiveness.
- Owner's representatives have different levels of involvement in a building project, ranging from representing the owner in the design phase through completion of the construction.
- Individuals with experience as architects, engineers, or construction managers make excellent owner's representatives.
- Owner's representatives help congregations save money while getting the highest possible quality.

Questions for Your Team

1. If members of your team have had new houses built, invite them to share a brief experience they have had monitoring and ensuring the quality of their new house.
2. Ask your team to discuss what they view as the benefits of an owner's representative for the building project your congregation is about to undertake.
3. In light of the level of complexity of your proposed project, discuss with your team options your congregation has for oversight that ensures the quality of your building project.

Conclusion

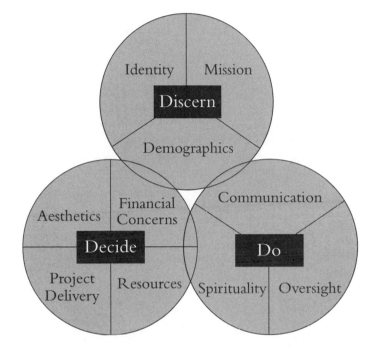

*I*t's moving day. Congregation Etz Chaim is relocating from their old sanctuary to their new one. It's raining, but the rain doesn't stop them. Driving by, you see a large crowd of people marching to their new spiritual home. You see a banner carried by two men. It reads *Hanukat Ha Bayit*, which means *Dedication of the Home*. You notice the people carrying the large container that holds the Torah, the Jewish Scriptures. They aren't going empty-handed to their new Canaan.

An hour ago the new sanctuary was empty. Now it is full of worshipers, old and young alike. Full of life. The liturgy is one of thanks.

Photos taken this day show people with attentive faces happily packed into this new space. This is a day of celebration. The work is done. It is as if the community looks back at their creation and says, "It is good."

Like Etz Chaim, you will come to the end of your building project. Maybe your congregation also is building a new sanctuary. Or perhaps you are renovating a basement or adding to your education space. Whatever your project, it is important to celebrate. Just as with other aspects of your building project, you will want to celebrate in a way that is consistent with your congregational culture. You may celebrate in the sanctuary with a full liturgy. Or you may instead have a feast. Or both. People not only enjoy breaking bread together around a celebration, but it gives sacred space project leaders a chance to thank others.

The key to celebration is gratitude. Thank everyone. Make sure you include the youngest and oldest members of your faith community. Celebration is thanksgiving. How does your congregation offer thanks? Some that we have worked with decorate grandly for such celebrations with banners, balloons, flowers, and colorful table settings. Like a family poring over a picture album, others show slides or photos of the building project. Some tell stories of how the faith community came together or share testimonies of God's part in the project.

Celebration is important because a building project is hard work. If you followed the discern, decide, do process, you gave this project the attention it deserved. During the *discern* phase, you asked hard questions. Your sacred space team sought to understand what God was communicating through your building and how you could reach out to your neighbors. During the *decide* phase, you made choices about aesthetics, project delivery, resources, and funding. During the *do* phase, you made sure that good communication, faithful attention to spirituality, and proper project oversight were taking place. These things didn't happen automatically. They required your time and your best effort. So it is good to celebrate.

Building projects take time—most longer than planned. Celebrating means not only giving thanks, but also remembering where and when you started and your journey from then to now. It is important to reflect on the passage of time. Too often congregational life mirrors the cultural desire to solve difficult things quickly and with as little pain as possible. A true celebration of a building project not only celebrates the improvements to sacred space, but it also lifts up the value of taking the time to do something well. A job well done is often one that takes time.

One leader we know finished speaking at a celebration dinner for a new kitchen. It now fed more than three hundred homeless people every week. As he finished with his thank-yous, which had taken a long time, there was a moment of silence. From the silence, a voice from one of the tables said aloud, "Thank you, God!" Another voice spoke up, this time toward the person who had led the project. People heard, "And thank you!"

What a fine image for a congregation and a fine image for what an effective building project can do for a faith community. You build a home for a community of thanksgiving; a kind and generous people work through difficult things and come through with a chorus of thank yous. At the end of the project, you have become like a religious order that gathers to recite antiphonally the Psalms back and forth to one another. Only here the psalm is a simple one. A chorus of thank-yous sounds through the new bricks and mortar that make up the house of God.

As you finish the building project and wrap up the celebration, remember that no building is ever complete. Like a gospel that ends in midsentence or a rabbinic discussion over a text that isn't solved, your congregation will leave the celebration and notice something that still needs to be done. Perhaps the stairs aren't wide enough. Or maybe the narthex is the wrong color for these times. One project leads to another. In fact, we have heard of at least one congregation that purposely left their new sanctuary unfinished as a sign that the building was not the whole story. What buildings do is help move the story forward. They reinforce a congregation's purpose. And that purpose is always unfolding, building, breaking new ground for the sake of a people, a local community and, yes, even the world.

APPENDIX A Facilities Assessments

*H*ow much longer will our roof last? Are we using the most efficient heating and cooling system? What are the first steps to begin the renovation process on that old education wing?

Congregations are often full of questions about how best to maintain and repair their sacred spaces. From the nuts and bolts of a good electrical system to the more abstract concepts of planning space for the future, a full assessment of the facility and all of its parts is an invaluable tool for congregations.

What Is a Facilities Assessment?

Aliases. Although known by many names—*facilities survey, conditions assessment, conditions survey, facilities audit,* or *conditions audit*—the facilities assessment is a holistic overview of your facility's condition by an appropriate team of professionals who assess the current condition of the building and its components.

Maintaining history. Those wanting to repair a historical building or to restore it to its original splendor may want to invest in a historic structure report. This type of facilities assessment goes into the history of the building and arrives at the original materials used and tells how the building has evolved or been altered through the years. In this report, the assessor uses history as a basis for making decisions about the future and to find the most appropriate way to repair or restore the building.

Assessing and planning. A master plan report is another type of facilities assessment. To complete this report, the assessor looks at the future space uses of the building. This report incorporates strategic planning aspects into the assessment.

Why Do We Need a Facilities Assessment?

Bird's-eye view. Facilities assessments take a wide view of facilities. Congregations need to know the condition of their existing facilities so they can best make decisions and plans for the future. It is not cost efficient to respond to problems one at a time. All systems in a building interact, so it makes sense to consider their overall, as well as individual, needs.

Better planning. Congregations can better apply their resources if they have the whole picture. Knowing the size and scope of a repair project assists with fundraising, planning, scheduling, and other aspects.

Focus your energy. Congregations want to make the most of what they have. A facilities assessment lets you know where you need work. If you know what parts of the building are in good condition, you can maintain those areas with minimal effort and put your energies into the areas that need attention. The assessment helps you to be more time and cost efficient. The results can sometimes be surprising. It is worth the cost to get a clear picture of your buildings' needs.

Staying or moving? A congregation considering a move may want to invest in a facilities assessment. An audit of your current location can be an important component in making this difficult decision.

Ongoing assessment. Be an "educated consumer" by performing your own ongoing facility assessment. Even the sturdiest of buildings needs regular maintenance and repair. Ongoing assessment involves checklists of needed tasks, keeping up on required maintenance, being aware of emerging problems, and organizing a small committee to regularly discuss maintenance concerns. Congregations can save time and money by knowing their buildings and keeping up on the issues. A five-hundred-dollar problem can quickly escalate into a five-thousand-dollar or even a fifty-thousand-dollar problem if it is not addressed in a timely fashion.

Who Does Facilities Assessment?

Leading the charge. Most facilities assessments are led by an architect but are performed by a team of professionals with expertise in the areas of heating and cooling, electrical, flooring, roofing, windows, structure, etc. The building assessor assigns the various components of the building to the person with the appropriate knowledge.

Finding your assessor. Congregations can search a variety of sources to find the right person for the job. Check with other congregations, your denominational office, local historical groups, or local nonprofit organizations.

Narrow the field. Once you have recommendations from the above sources, begin sorting through those whom you would like to interview. Look for assessors who have qualifications and experience with buildings or facilities like yours. Interview at least three of the candidates and check references. Then trust your instincts and choose the person who has "chemistry" with your congregation.

Are We Ready for an Assessment?

The committee. Have a committee or team in place to work with your chosen building consultant. This group should be made up of about eight people—small enough to be manageable but not so small that its members are easily overworked. Team members don't have to have construction or maintenance knowledge. Anyone who is dedicated and passionate about the congregation makes a great addition to the committee.

Select a spokesperson. Appoint one team member to be the communicator for the committee. Frustration can mount if the assessor is getting instructions from many different sources.

Be prepared. The more information you can provide to the assessor, the less expensive and more complete the assessment will be. Have ready any drawings or blueprints of the building, including additions, maintenance records, historical documentation, photographs, and records of any renovation or restoration. No matter how old the documents, they are still helpful. Even if the information is not in hand, it is valuable to find it through your local historical society, previous contractors, state or county offices, or denominational office. If enough historical or maintenance data is not available, architects sometimes have to do "exploratory demolition" to investigate what is going on within the structure. This involves breaking through the walls or roof or other areas to investigate and gather the needed information. It is worth spending additional time to find documentation.

Communicate. Keeping open lines of communication is key to any project. The congregation and governing boards need to be kept up to date on the progress of, reasons for, and results of the assessment. The team working with the assessor needs to feel comfortable talking with one another and with the architect. A smooth give-and-take with the assessor makes his or her job easier and keeps everyone informed throughout the process.

We Have an Assessment, Now What Do We Do?

Study the report. It is best if the assessor walks the maintenance or capital project committee through his or her findings and recommendations. The assessor can answer questions and provide additional explanation if needed. Most consultants will be glad to do this.

Spread the word. Let the congregation know what is in the assessment—areas that need work, recommendations, and cost estimates. The information may be surprising to members. It may take some time to process the information before it is accepted and members are ready to begin the planning phase.

Plan of action. The final report usually includes phasing or staging the work that needs to be done, based on the information the congregation provided about the availability and timing of funds. Once the congregation is comfortable with the scope and cost of the project, the assessor can develop a plan, help locate good contractors for the congregation to consider, and oversee the work once contracts are signed and the project begins.

File the report in a safe place. Keep the assessment report for future reference. It will be helpful during the project and later on if more work needs to be done. It will also be useful historical documentation for the next assessment.

A typical facilities assessment will include most of the following:

- introduction
- brief history of construction and maintenance
- summary of findings
- description of existing conditions
- causes of problems
- recommendations and remarks
- cost estimates
- photographs
- drawings, sketch or measured
- optional reports from various specialists, such as structural engineer, stained-glass consultant, mechanical or electrical engineer, etc.

Learn More

Goldberg, Shari P. *Managing Repair and Restoration Projects: A Congregation's How-to Guide.* New York: New York Landmark Conservancy, 2002. This resource is written specifically for laypeople working to preserve their houses of worship. It offers step-by-step details for assessing the building, planning the work, handling contracts, and overseeing construction, including an example on page 52 of a conditions survey. The book includes other sample documents as well, along with a glossary and a list of resources.

Lovejoy, Kim. "Special Report: Building Conditions Surveys," *Common Bond* magazine, June 1998, http://www.sacredplaces. org/PSP-InfoClearingHouse/articles/Special%20Report.htm. This informative article found on the Partners for Sacred Places Web site discusses the facilities assessment. The article addresses the scope of the survey, funding the assessment, finding a consultant, communicating the results, and more.

Partners for Sacred Places. www.sacredplaces.org. Partners for Sacred Places is a nonprofit organization devoted to helping Americans care for and make good use of older and historic religious properties. Partners maintains an information clearinghouse, accessible from its Web site, which contains extensive building-related resources. Many of the resources are available free online. Partners also publishes resources related to property maintenance and fundraising.

Sources for this appendix include A. Robert Jaeger and Tuomi Forrest of Partners for Sacred Places; Jerry Cripps of InterDesign; Kevin Rose of Cumberland First Baptist Church, Cumberland, Indiana; and Kim Lovejoy, "Special Report: Building Conditions Surveys," Common Bond *magazine, June 1998.*

APPENDIX B Selecting Fundraisers

*F*undraising can be a touchy and difficult issue for congregations. Growth, expansion, remodeling, and repairs often require a religious organization to focus on the money necessary to most successfully continue its ministry and spiritual education. Professional fundraising consultants can put their experience and expertise to work, bringing a sense of accomplishment, community, and fulfillment to a congregation's stewardship efforts.

Tips for Selecting a Fundraising Consultant

Get a little help from your friends. Ask around and find out whom other congregations hired as their fundraising consultants. What did they think of that person or firm? What were the pros and cons of working with that particular fundraiser? Their thoughts and comments can help you decide which consulting firms to consider.

Does your denomination provide fundraisers? Keep in mind that many denominations have in-house fundraising consultants. These professionals can often help your congregation with the beginning stages of planning or even take you through the entire campaign, depending on the size of your plan and their time and abilities.

Let your fingers do the walking. Once you decide on a few fundraising consultants whom you would like to consider, contact them and ask that they send you some preliminary information. Find out what kinds of services they provide. Once you have this information, decide which fundraisers you would like to interview and set up a face-to-face meeting.

Meeting face-to-face. There are a variety of interview approaches, depending upon the fundraiser with whom you are working. Some believe you should talk to the person who will actually be working with your congregational leaders on the fundraising campaign. Others send a salesperson or field representative to the initial interview to provide general information and then encourage a second interview with a specific fundraising consultant from their organization. Either way, it is important that your leaders meet with the prospective consultant in person before making the decision to hire that fundraiser.

Look for a good "fit" when choosing your consultant. Consultants and congregational leaders agree that a positive chemistry between congregational leaders and their fundraiser is imperative for a comfortable working relationship and successful campaign. Look for someone who understands and fits with the culture of your congregation.

Help the consultant to see your vision. Let your prospective fundraisers know your plans and vision for the future. The size of your project directly impacts the size of your capital campaign. Some consultants and firms specialize in various types of fundraising efforts. Information given up front can help you find the best match for your particular needs.

Experience, experience, experience. Both knowledge of and experience in fundraising are musts. Capital campaigns in religious organizations are different than other nonprofit groups. Some experts even recommend looking for someone with experience with your particular denomination and demographics.

Look for someone who can communicate trust. A congregation and its leaders need to feel a high degree of trust in the consultant. Find someone who makes you feel confident in his or her leadership, honesty, and integrity.

Consultant needs to understand you. He or she needs to understand who you are as a congregation. Excellent consultants will be willing to work with your congregation's individuality rather than trying to put you in a prepressed mold.

Keep the dialogue flowing. Communication must come easily between the congregational leaders and the consultant. Look for someone who will keep you informed and listen to your needs and concerns.

How do they rate? When choosing a fundraising consultant, be sure to obtain written and oral references. Other clients' experiences are usually telling as to the way the consultant does business.

Beware of commissions. Look for a consultant who charges a flat fee for his or her services. Beware of those who charge a percentage or bonus. The fundraiser should be able to tell you his or her fee up front.

Know the costs. Once you know the fee, find out when it is due. How does the consultant wish to be paid? Can payments be made in installments? Does the fee include travel and expenses? Does it include the feasibility study?

Who is doing what? Fundraising consultants differ in the services they provide. Find out just what the consultant plans to do and what he or she expects the congregation to do. Clearly defined duties will help you determine if this is the fundraiser for you and will minimize surprises down the road.

Feasibility study. Some fundraising consultants conduct a feasibility study to reveal the congregation's fundraising capacity. Find out if the consultants you are considering will conduct a feasibility study and how. You need to know how the consultant plans to study and compile this information. Other fund consultants believe that feasibility studies are detrimental to a fund campaign because they sway the focus to money rather than ministry. How does your congregation feel about a feasibility study?

Helping you to help yourself. A good fund consultant will help the congregation take ownership of the fundraising campaign. Involving many members and attendees from throughout your congregation will raise enthusiasm and give new life to the campaign and to your ministry.

On-the-job training and education. Look for a consultant who will provide training and help equip congregational leaders with the skills necessary to conduct the fundraising campaign.

It's not cheap, but it's worth it. Hiring a professional fundraiser can be expensive, but the benefits far exceed the cost. Congregations that hire fundraising consultants usually enjoy a successful campaign. Some say that they were amazed at how much money and enthusiasm were raised. They would not have anticipated that before working with their professional fundraising consultant.

Questions to Ask a Fundraising Firm

How is the invitation to give presented to the congregation?
How do you as a consultant get to know the congregation?
How is the standard methodology adapted to accommodate the
   unique qualities of the congregation?

What is your approach to feasibility studies that determine how much a congregation can raise? Do you conduct them, and if so, how?

What kind of follow-up work will you provide after the campaign is completed? Is there an additional cost for follow-up work?

How are the roles of the consultant and the congregational leadership defined?

What is the fee structure—a flat fee or a percentage of the campaign goal? Are expenses included in the fee? What is the payment schedule?

Provide a list of references from the past two years—three successful congregational campaigns and one failure and their campaign financial goals. (Failure may be that the congregation resigned from the process.)

Learn More

Dean, Peggy Powell, and Susanna A. Jones. *The Complete Guide to Capital Campaigns for Historic Churches and Synagogues*. Philadelphia: Partners for Sacred Places, 1998. Focused on capital campaigns for historic religious buildings, this loose-leaf notebook includes an outline of the capital campaign process, plus advice on involving community leaders not affiliated with the congregation.

Holliman, Glen N., and Barbara L. Holliman. *With Generous Hearts: How to Raise Capital Funds for Your Church, Church School, Church Agency or Regional Church Body*. Harrisburg, PA: Morehouse, 1997. This book is an excellent overview of capital campaigns. The Hollimans, who are capital campaign consultants, emphasize the importance of a thorough feasibility study and the need for advanced gifts. They present six steps of effective fundraising.

Information for this appendix is provided by David McDonald of Advent, Inc.; Clif Christopher of Horizons Stewardship Co., LLC; Tommy Blakely of Resource Services, Inc.; Jessica White of Jessica White Associates; Rev. Craig Parker of Bridgeway Community Church, Fishers, Indiana; Rev. Mike Reed of Fishers United Methodist Church, Fishers, Indiana; Rev. Tom True of First United Methodist Church, Shelbyville, Indiana; and Rev. Karen Devaisher and Bill Pfaffenberger of Avon United Methodist Church, Avon, Indiana.

APPENDIX C Working with an Architect

Working successfully with an architect depends on cooperation, thoughtful consideration, prayerful planning, research, and adherence to timelines and budgets. Although challenges are inherent to any architectural project, these barriers can be minimized with good planning, open lines of communication, and an ongoing awareness of the true goals of the project.

Following is a list of pointers from architects and congregational leaders to assist those embarking on the winding road of architectural planning.

Discuss what is driving this project. Be sure a project is being considered for the right reasons. Sometimes dissatisfaction with the current facility can be a sign that other problems exist in the congregation—the inadequacy of the building is just one problem that everyone can agree upon.

Look at the real needs of the congregation. Work with your architect to evaluate your congregation's needs. Sometimes a critical review helps identify the next step.

Consider all aspects of your ministry. When planning for the new building, remember to consider the worship area, classrooms, fellowship hall, offices, acoustics, entrances and exits, parking, and presentation to passersby.

Always plan for the future. When considering a facility change, count on your architect to help you look toward future growth. Don't just think about what is needed now, but consider what may be needed ten years from now.

Know how much money can be spent. Know up front what the congregation can spend. Be sure to let the architect know this immediately. Establish priorities and set acceptable budgetary ranges.

Check with your neighbors. Let the experiences of others help you. Visit other area congregational facilities to see what you like and don't like about their buildings. Find those that "feel right" and contact the architects. Talk to people from other congregations who have recently been through building projects. Their knowledge and advice can help with new ideas and better understanding.

Rely upon your architects to maneuver through a complex arena. These professionals have extensive experience in the building industry. Architects know how to solve problems creatively. They often look beyond the walls and windows to find creative solutions and the best design and environment for you.

Select your architect with care. Interview and hire professionals. You will work with your architect for a long time, so put thoughtful consideration into the choosing.

Know your architect's plans and practices. Ask each potential architect about his or her design philosophy. Find out how the architect plans to go about information gathering on your project. Ask how priorities are established and decisions made. These questions can help you determine who is the best candidate for the job.

Let your architect help select a contractor. The choice of contractor is largely based on the construction documents prepared by the architect, so be sure to take the architect's opinion into consideration when making this choice.

Get your architect on board right away. Congregations sometimes wait too long to contact an architect. These professionals can give good advice on items such as zoning, utilities, land purchases, etc., early in the process.

Help the architect understand your congregation. Invite your architect to attend worship. The architect can best accommodate your needs if he or she grasps the concepts of your worship and what occurs in your building.

Let the congregation meet the architect. Plan an all-congregation meeting with the architect. Let him or her present the building process with support from building committee members. Ask for feedback from parishioners in writing.

Timelines keep your project on track. It is important to discuss the timing of the project. Be sure to target a completion date. Without these aspects, the project could linger.

The architect's services don't stop when construction begins. Your architect should continue to take an active role in your project, even after the construction phase begins. He or she can work closely with the contractor, evaluate the work, make necessary design changes, and inspect the completed facility.

Communication is the key to a successful project. Communication is a must. Talk about the vision of the project, let everyone know why time and money are being spent, ask for clarification of architectural and building terms, get ideas from the staff and all facets of the congregation, and don't hesitate to ask questions if anything is unclear. Leaders need to have a strong voice if the project is to reflect the congregation's values, needs, and personality.

Clear responsibilities should be defined. All parties of the building project have specific and important jobs. These functions and expectations need to be clearly outlined and understood.

Beware of false expectations. A new or remodeled facility will not get the congregation more involved in ministry or cause them to give more in contributions, nor will it automatically increase attendance.

Beginning a building project is a huge undertaking for a congregation. It requires a financial and emotional commitment. But the results can be vastly rewarding when the project is ministry driven and stays true to its calling.

A building project that begins with good financial planning, widespread communication, and a spiritual perspective can result in a renewed facility, allowing the congregation to move ahead and focus on other positive spiritual issues.

Architectural Services Available★

Project Administration and Management

- Disciplines coordination and document checking
- Schedule development and monitoring of the work
- Construction management

Evaluation and Planning Services

- Existing facilities surveys
- Site analysis, selection, and development planning
- On-site and off-site utility studies
- Zoning process assistance

Design Services

- Architectural design/documentation
- Structural design/documentation

- Mechanical design/documentation
- Electrical design/documentation
- Civil design/documentation
- Landscape design/documentation
- Interior design/documentation

Bidding or Negotiation Services

- Bid evaluation
- Contract award

Contract Administration Services

- Full-time, on-site project representative
- Testing and inspection administration
- Furniture and equipment installation administration

*Adapted from "You and Your Architect" (New York: American Association of Architects, 2001), www.aia.org/consumer/youandyourarchitect. pdf.

Learn More

Church Architecture: A Network of Information for Building and Renovating, www.churcharchitecture.net, is a service of Dixon Studios. It is a guide to resources for church building and renovation and includes articles and books about architectural issues and a variety of links to other helpful building-related websites.

"You and Your Architect," American Institute of Architects, www. aia.org/consumer/youandyourarchitect.pdf. This article includes information about the services of architects; advice for selecting an architect, negotiating a contract, and keeping your project on track; and other valuable hints for making your involvement with an architect successful.

Information for this appendix is provided by Sherry Perkins, operating director of Connection Pointe Christian Church of Brownsburg, Brownsburg, Indiana; Jerry Cripps, InterDesign; Tim Fleck, Woollen Molzan and Partners, Inc.; Mike Eagan, Entheos Architects; Barney Boyd, Byron Stuart Boyd and Associates; Michael Cope, MECA Design Group; Jim McQuiston, J.W. McQuiston Architect; Steve Robinson, Browning Day Mullins Dierdorf, Inc.; "Selecting an Architect," www.aiacorpuschristi.org; "Working with an Architect," www.andersonarchitects.com; "What You Should Know about Working with an Architect," www.jkadesign.net.

Architectural Firm Analysis

	Architect Firms					Design/Build Firms		
Firm								
Address								
City, State								
Contact								
Phone								
Fax								
E-mail								
Web site								
Firm's design staff size								
# of years in business								
# of years in congregation designs								
% of congregation business in this geographic area								
# of congregation projects in the last five years								
Projects of interest in the area								

APPENDIX D Relating to Contractors

A construction project is a huge undertaking for a congregation. Plans, architects, contractors, blueprints, and budgets are just a few of the many intricate facets involved. Developing and maintaining a good relationship with the contractor who will build your project can help smooth the road to a successful and meaningful outcome.

Have processes in place. Appoint a building committee, decide how decisions will be made, and stick to the plan. When issues arise, they can be easily funneled through the already-familiar process, allowing for a timely resolution. Building projects require numerous decisions, so it is important to set up a plan early. The road won't always be smooth, but having a set process in place can help the congregation and the contractor avoid frustrating dilemmas.

Know what you want. By the time you begin looking for a contractor, you need to have in mind what you want your building project to include and how much money you can afford to spend. Be decisive. You may be dealing with a variety of ideas from a number of people, but you must present a unified plan so that your contractor will be better able to serve your needs.

Find a contractor who is right for you. Talk to your architect and to other congregations who have completed building projects. Do some research. Check references. Find someone with experience in church construction. Recognize that there are many good contractors, but not every contractor is right for every project. Find the one who is best suited to your needs. Always beware of nepotism. It is fine to consider hiring the pastor's son as your contractor, but be sure you are considering him in the same light as the other candidates.

Take a proactive approach. Do a little homework to find out all you can about the construction process. If you know how things work in the construction business, terms used and common practices, you will be better equipped to choose and work with your contractor.

Bring your contractor on board early. Finding a contractor early in the process can be the key to a successful building project. This allows the contractor, congregation, and architect to work together as a team. You can set up common expectations and become unified in your purpose. The contractor can provide advice on time frames, costs, materials, and scheduling up front. In the end, this step can help control costs.

Develop a good relationship. It is essential that the contractor and congregation build a level of trust. To do this, the building committee and contractor need to work closely together and get to know one another. Common experiences build trust. This is another good reason to bring your contractor into the project early.

Choose a point person. Appoint one person to be the spokesperson for the congregation's construction committee. Frustration will mount if the contractor is getting instructions from many different sources.

Communication is the key. Keep the lines of communication open. Set up a weekly meeting or walk-through with your contractor and communicate often. Telephone and e-mail are great tools, but face-to-face meetings are imperative. Get to know your project manager or job superintendent, who are on the work site most of the time monitoring progress. Let your contractor know of any obstacles or special requests. If you are renovating, be sure the contractor knows what areas of the building are being used and when so that he or she can schedule work when it is most convenient.

Ask a lot of questions. Never hesitate to ask for clarification. Contractors often use terms that are understood in the construction field but are foreign to the average congregational leader. Ask them to speak your language so that you are confident that you understand everything. Avoiding misunderstandings can save time, money, and peace of mind.

Make a list and check it twice. Keep a running list of questions and issues that you want to discuss with your contractor. As the questions are answered and the tasks completed, check them off, noting the date. Doing so will keep you updated on the progress and remind you that something has or has not been completed. Ask the contractor to do the same, including providing a progress report with the billing.

Expect the unexpected. Construction is not an exact science. Many parts and pieces and components have to come together to make a building work. You will face some surprises and unexpected issues. Be prepared emotionally and financially for these. Being aware and ready makes the process run more smoothly.

Consider hiring some help. Another option for congregations is hiring an owner's representative or owner's advocate. This is a person or company well versed in the construction business who acts as a liaison between the congregation and the contractor. He or she will help you understand the timelines, terms, blueprints and details of the work.

The importance of a successful finish. Do a final walk-through with your contractor to be sure everything is in order. Be sure you are provided with the closing construction documents and instructions on maintenance. It will be important to know how to clean and maintain that new floor in the entryway, or how to operate the new dishwasher in the kitchen. A one-year or six-month walk-through is also recommended. The building may shift in time, requiring some additional work or repairs. A good closing is the perfect end to a successful project.

Learn More

Elliott, Jon. *Disaster Prevention Guide for Church Building Projects.* Oxnard, CA: Church Growth Institute, 2003. This comprehensive overview of what is involved in congregational building projects comes in a three-ring binder with two accompanying CDs. The focus of this resource is on planning, including the funding plan, design plan, management plan, schedule, and communications plan.

Goldberg, Shari P. *Managing Repair and Restoration Projects: A Congregation's How-to Guide.* New York: New York Landmarks Conservancy, Inc., 2002. Written specifically for laypeople working to preserve their historical houses of worship, this resource offers step-by-step details for building assessment, planning, handling contracts, and overseeing construction. An appendix includes sample documents, a glossary, and a list of resources.

PraiseBuildings. www.churchconstruction.com. This Web site provides a well-organized annotated guide to resources and specialists in church construction and facilitation, including denominational resources.

Information for this appendix was provided by Andy Corman, First Presbyterian in Noblesville, Indiana, and AnCor Construction Services; Jerry Cripps, InterDesign; Michael Engledow, Schmidt Architects; Ken Hatch, Church at the Crossing, Indianapolis; Todd Mattingly, Brandt Construction; Brian Smith, Trader's Point Christian Church, Indianapolis; and Carl Sutherly, Wurster Construction Co.

APPENDIX E Sacred Space Grants Initiative

Since its inception in 1997, the Indianapolis Center for Congregations has worked with congregations on more than three hundred occasions concerning building issues. These issues included building expansion and renovation funding, relocation, architectural design, interior design, special usage (e.g., senior centers and youth rooms), energy efficiency, congregations with buildings on lots that didn't leave room for expansion, and many more. As part of our work in late 2003, the Center began our Sacred Space Grants Initiative (SSGI). SSGI was designed to help congregations address the challenges of matching their building's space with their mission.

Congregations selected for the program participated in a Sacred Space course consisting of four class sessions. The classes were designed to help participants learn how to lead an effective building project. The congregations also received on-site visits from knowledgeable consultants who helped them assess their present circumstances and consider how to take the next steps toward improving or expanding their sacred space. They then developed a sacred space plan customized to accomplish their ministry goals and were given the opportunity to submit a proposal for a grant to help with the cost of implementing the sacred space plan they conceived. The grants were limited to thirty thousand dollars, which had to be matched dollar for dollar by the congregation. Only congregations that completed the required coursework and consultations and developed a sacred space plan could make grant proposals.

More than three hundred congregations attended information meetings about the grants program. One hundred and twenty-five applied. Fifty-one were admitted into the program.

When the Center for Congregations created SSGI to teach congregations how to think about how their buildings affect their ministries, our primary goal was to provide a broad background of what is available for critically thinking congregations. Center staff developed the SSGI based on their work with building issues and congregations. They also worked with a number of curriculum partners to develop a comprehensive program.[1]

During the development of SSGI, we created a new model to help congregations think wisely and well about their sacred spaces. We called this model *discern, decide, and do*. Each phase of the model—discern, decide, and do—consists of a series of questions a congregation must address.

The discern, decide, and do model is not rigidly linear. That is, it does not have to move sequentially from discern to decide to do. The center's work has shown that congregational building projects often involve some discernment followed by decisions, more discernment, then doing, then more discernment and more deciding. Since the process is not linear, the important thing is to be aware of opportunities for discerning and deciding while doing or doing while deciding or any of the combination of the three steps that fits your needs and culture.

Another component that made SSGI unique and successful grew out of one of the great learnings from the center's first major grants program, the Computers and Ministry Grants Program. CMGI showed the value of having a team develop a technology plan. This team approach was unique in that it was not a team of technology-oriented people. Rather, it was a team composed of representatives of vital ministry areas—worship, youth, pastoral care, and so on. This team focused on ministry first, then asked how technology could (or could not) enhance their ministry. One of the benefits that we saw to this approach was that it could be used in other congregational problem solving or planning areas. That is why we applied it, with equal effectiveness, to the SSGI program. Each congregation that participated in SSGI named a sacred space team to attend the classes and participate in the design of the congregation's sacred space plan and final grant submission.

We found that 90 percent of the SSGI congregations that worked through our discern, decide, and do model used a sacred space team. And those that made prayerful, thoughtful, and intentional use of each area of the model ended the SSGI program with a solid plan for matching their facility with their mission. The program was so successful that the Center awarded more than $1.5 million dollars in matching grants for the implementation of sacred space plans.

Glossary

*B*uilding issues have a language of their own. While some of the terms vary from region to region and vendor to vendor, the following list provides some of the most commonly agreed upon words and phrases. This list is an amalgamation of building-related words and phrases, including some unique to this book. It was developed in part from a glossary by Jerry Cripps of InterDesign for our Sacred Space Grant Initiative and from sources such as www. homebuildingmanual.com and http://www.contractorslicense. com/0-24-glossary.htm.

A/C. An abbreviation for air conditioner or air-conditioning.

addendum, addenda (pl.). A written or pictorial document by an architect, prepared prior to signing a construction contract, that modifies the bidding documents by making additions, deletions, clarifications, or corrections.

additional services (of the architect). Services that, after authorization by an owner, are performed by an architect in addition to the basic services spelled out in the original contract.

allowance(s). A dollar amount designated for items not selected and/or specified in a construction contract. For example, an electrical allowance sets the amount of money to be spent on electrical fixtures.

alternate. Possible change(s) described in the contract documents that gives an owner the option to choose alternative materials, products, or systems or to add or delete segments of work.

application for payment. A contractor's request for payment for work completed, and if allowed by the contract, for materials or equipment to be used in work.

architect. A person who has completed a course of study in building and design and is licensed as an architect.

base bid. Amount of money in a bid as the figure for which the bidder offers to perform the work depicted in the bid documents.

basic services (of the architect). An architect's basic services are made up of the stages described in an owner-architect agreement. These often include schematic designs, design development, bidding, construction documents, and construction administration.

bearing wall. A wall that supports a load in addition to its own weight.

bidding or negotiation phase. The time period when competitive bids and/or proposals are received for a project.

blue stake (utility notification). When a utility company (telephone, gas, electric, cable TV, sewer, or water, etc.) or their contracted service provider comes to a job site and marks the location of underground utilities.

builder's risk insurance. Insurance coverage on a project during construction.

building permit. Written authorization from the city, county, or other governing regulatory body giving permission to construct or renovate a building.

certificate for payment. A report from the architect to the owner confirming the amount of money payable to the contractor for completed work or materials and equipment purchased.

certificate of occupancy. Document issued by a governmental power officially stating that all or part of a building is approved for its designated use.

change order. A modification to the construction contract that authorizes a change in the work.

commissioning. Bringing a building's mechanical and electrical systems online by testing or through other action in order to make sure that the equipment is operating as designed and installed. This stage also typically involves developing operation and maintenance manuals and providing systems training for the owner.

conditions assessment. A thorough inspection by an architectural firm or other facility expert, such as a commercial inspector or structural or civil engineer to determine a building's condition.

construction budget. The sum established as available for construction of the project (distinguishable from the project budget).

construction cost. The total estimated cost of all elements of the project designed or specified by the architect.

construction documents. Drawings and specifications that delineate the specific requirements for construction of a project.

construction management. Project delivery method that consists of hiring a construction manger to oversee an entire project and coordinate between the owner, architect, and contractor. It is most useful for complex projects requiring a lot of planning, scheduling, and coordination.

contractor. A company or person licensed to perform particular types of construction activities, such as electrical, plumbing, etc. Some contractor licenses require specialized training, testing, and insurance.

demographics. Population characteristics, such as race, age, income, education, home ownership, employment status, household size, and so on for a defined area.

design-bid-build. Traditional project delivery method that consists of hiring an architect to create a design, inviting contractors to submit bids to construct the design, and then hiring one of the bidders to construct the building.

design-build. The second most common project delivery method. It consists of a single firm doing both the design and the construction.

design development documents. Drawings and other documents that set the scope of the project's architectural, structural, mechanical, and electrical systems, materials, and other requirements.

draw. An amount of money that is available to a contractor under a contract that features a fixed payment schedule.

easement. A legal contract that gives one party use of a portion of another party's property for a specific purpose—for example, a sewer easement gives the right to run a sewer line through a neighboring property.

general contractor. A company or individual responsible for execution, supervision, and overall coordination of a project. While a general contractor may perform some construction tasks, many general contractors are not licensed to perform specialty trades and so hire specialty contractors for tasks such as electrical and plumbing.

guaranteed maximum price (GMP). A sum established by the owner and contractor as the maximum amount the owner will pay the contractor for performing specified work.

inspection list (punch list). A list of items of work to be completed or corrected by the contractor near the end of a project.

learning resources. Resources used for the specific purpose of learning about congregational building ventures.

lowest responsible bidder. Bidder who submits the lowest bid and is considered by the owner and the architect to be fully responsible and qualified to perform the work for which the bid is submitted.

master plan. A vision for the future development of property and facilities regarding site development and potential of the property.

mechanics lien. A lien on property in favor of the company or contractor who supplied labor or materials for a building.

mission statement. A statement that expresses a congregation's primary purpose.

negotiated select team. Project delivery method that involves the construction firm being hired before the project is designed. The contractor then attends and participates in all design meetings with the architect and congregation.

observation of the work. Examination by an architect of the work during recurring visits to the site. The purpose is to determine if the work is being completed as specified in the contract documents.

owner's representative (owner's inspector, clerk of the works). Person hired by the owner to inspect construction on the owner's behalf.

package builder. A builder that provides pre-designed, pre-engineered and manufactured steel buildings.

payment bond. A bond that guarantees the owner that the contractor will pay for labor and materials furnished for use as specified in the contract.

performance bond. A bond that guarantees the owner that the contractor's work will be performed in accordance with the contract.

permit. Governmental authorization to execute a building process such as zoning, demolition, usage, grading, septic, building, and so on.

predesign services. Services of an architect prior to basic services. Such services might include assisting the owner in determining financial and time requirements and limitations for the project.

preliminary design (design-build). Architect's services performed under the first part of an agreement of a design-build project. These include program review, preliminary program evaluation, and review of alternative approaches to design and construction and preliminary design documents.

preliminary design documents (design-build). Preliminary design drawings, specifications, and other documents that describe the total nature of a design-build project, including architectural, structural, mechanical, and electrical systems, as well as materials.

preliminary estimate of construction cost. Cost forecasts by the architect for the owner during the design development and construction documents stages of basic services.

project budget. The amount of funds set by the owner as available for the entire project, including construction costs, furniture, furnishings and equipment, financing costs, compensation for professional services, contingency allowance, and other costs. This is distinguished from the construction budget.

project creep. The numerous things added to a project as it progresses, thereby resulting in growing costs and extended time frames.

project delivery system. The method selected to accomplish the design, document preparation, construction, and management of a project.

proposal request. A document issued by the architect after contract award that may include drawings and other information used to solicit a proposal for a change to the work; sometimes called a request for a change or a bulletin.

punch list. See *inspection list*.

record drawings. Construction drawings revised to show changes made during the construction process, usually based on marked-up prints or drawings.

sacred space. Any part of a building or grounds used by a congregation or for programs hosted by that congregation.

sacred space team. A group of people charged with determining what a congregation wants to do in relation to a building project by enlisting the ideas and support of all aspects of a congregation.

schedule of values. A statement furnished by the contractor to the architect describing the portions of the contract that are allocated to the various portions of the work. It is used as the basis for reviewing a contractor's applications for payment.

schematic design documents. Drawings and other documents showing the scale and connection of project components.

shop drawings. Drawings, diagrams, schedules, and other data prepared by a contractor, subcontractor, manufacturer, supplier, or distributor that show some segment of the work.

specifications. A section of the contract documents consisting of written requirements for materials, equipment, construction systems, standards, and workmanship.

standard of care. The reasonable degree of care required of a prudent professional. This is the measure used in determining legal rights.

standard practices of the trade(s). Common basic and minimum construction standards.

subcontractor. A person or company that contracts directly with a general contractor to perform specified work.

substantial completion. The stage in the progress of a project when a designated portion of the building is sufficiently complete in accordance with the contract documents so that it can be occupied or utilized for its intended use.

value engineering. The process of studying the design elements in terms of cost effectiveness. This may include proposed substitution of less expensive materials or systems to replace those originally suggested.

APPENDIX G Resources

The Alban Institute
2121 Cooperative Way
Suite 100
Herndon, VA 20171
800-486-1318
www.alban.org

The Alban Institute is a not-for-profit organization that provides
consulting, educational events, and publishing related to congregational vitality. Consultants work with congregations in areas
such as visioning, strategic planning, congregational change, and
leadership development.

American Institute of Architects (AIA)
1735 New York Ave., NW
Washington, DC 20006-5292
800-AIA-3837 or 202-626-7300; Fax 202-626-7547
infocentral@aia.org

AIA is the national professional organization for architects. Many
states have local chapters that maintain offices and often an AIA

store. The AIA Web site provides helpful information regarding all facets of building and an architect locator to help you identify architects in your region of the country. The AIA sells preprinted contracts for all phases of construction. Users of the contracts fill in the blanks to fit their unique project.

Bowman, Ray, and Eddy Hall. *When Not to Build: An Architect's Un-conventional Wisdom for the Growing Church*. Expanded edition. Grand Rapids: Baker, 2000.

> This expanded edition includes a questionnaire to help congrega-tions assess their motivation for building and their readiness for a major building program. The book has three sections, which ad-dress focus (motivation), building use, and financial readiness.

Built of Living Stones: Art, Architecture, and Worship. Washington, DC: United States Conference of Catholic Bishops, 2000.

> This is the church building and renovation guide for Roman Catholic parishes in the United States. The first part examines each element of the physical structure in relationship to sacred rites and liturgy. Next comes a discussion of how art and the artist can assist the parish in worship. Finally, practical considerations are given concerning the roles of all engaged in the process.

Callahan, Kennon. *Building for Effective Mission: A Complete Guide for Congregations on Bricks and Mortar Issues*. San Francisco: Jossey-Bass, 1997.

> Callahan asserts that a congregation is a mission outpost to the people beyond its walls. In accordance with these principles,

this book describes concrete actions congregations may take to discover a mission and to plan for accomplishing it. Later chapters discuss the physical plant that furthers a chosen mission.

Chegwidden, Bill. *The Next Step: How to Discover the Right Solutions to Plan, Design, and Build Your Church*. Canton, GA: Riverstone Group, 2004.

Chegwidden, an architect who works exclusively with churches, has written a detailed guide for congregations planning a building project. He carefully describes land assessment and/or acquisition, relocation, project delivery methods, funding, and more. His book is rich with pictures of church campuses, both exteriors and interiors, making it not only informative, but also aesthetically pleasing. This resource is organized to help the reader access particular sections that are of most interest to them. Plenty of charts provide helpful summaries of the content. This book provides a good overview of the entire building process particularly for churches but useful to congregations of all faith traditions.

Church Architecture: A Resource Network
www.churcharchitecture.net

This Web site is a guide to resources for church building and renovation. It includes suppliers of such items as stained glass, lighting, furniture, and fonts as well as architects and liturgical consultants. It is well organized and nicely done, with many links for church-building enthusiasts to explore.

Clements, Patrick L. *Proven Concepts of Church Building and Finance: A Step-by-Step Guide to Successful Building Programs*. Grand Rapids: Kregel, 2002.

> How does a congregation begin and plan for building expansion, construction, or relocation? This guide provides pragmatic answers grounded in spiritual practices. With corporate prayer as foundation, the author explains how to obtain financing, establish a building committee, select a site, and work with architects and builders.

Crosbie, Michael J. *Architecture for the Gods*. New York: Watson-Guptill, 2000.

> A book of elaborate colored pictures, designs, and descriptions of forty new religious buildings representing Christian, Jewish, and Islamic faiths. Descriptions of each of the projects illustrate how the design emerged from the identity and needs of the congregation and how it communicates to the surrounding community.

Dean, Peggy Powell, and Susanna A. Jones. *The Complete Guide to Capital Campaigns for Historic Churches and Synagogues*. Philadelphia: Partners for Sacred Places, 1998.

> Capital campaigns to restore historic buildings offer opportunities to seek grants and gifts that are not ordinarily available to congregations. The two-hundred-page loose-leaf guide includes an outline of the capital campaign process that would be useful to any congregation, plus advice on involving community leaders not affiliated with the congregation and seeking grants from foundations and government sources.

Design-Build Institute of America
1100 H St., NW, Suite 500
Washington, DC 20005-5476
202-682-0110; Fax 202-682-5877
dbia@dbia.org

> DBIA is a membership organization that exists to promote the use of design-build as a project delivery method. Nonmembers can access their Web site, http://www.dbia.org/fr_publications.html, and find helpful free downloadable articles, such as "An Introduction to Design-Build" and "Design-Build Definitions." Congregations wishing to explore design-build as an option will find these free articles useful.

Elliott, Jon. *Disaster Prevention Guide for Church Building Projects*. Oxnard, CA: Church Growth Institute, 2003.

> This resource, in three-ring binder form with two accompanying audio compact discs, provides a comprehensive overview of what is involved in congregational building projects. The focus of the resource is on planning, including the funding plan, design plan, management plan, schedule, and communication plan.

Guide to Funding Ministry
http://www.guide-to-funding-ministry.net/great_links.html

> This Web site provides information and links about capital campaign consultants, direct mail fundraising, endowment and planned giving, and other subjects related to funding ministry.

Holliman, Glen N., and Barbara L. Holliman. *With Generous Hearts: How to Raise Capital Funds for Your Church, Church School, Church Agency or Regional Church Body*. Harrisburg, PA: Morehouse, 1997.

> This book is an excellent overview of capital campaigns. The Hollimans, who are capital campaign consultants, emphasize the importance of a thorough feasibility study and the need for advanced gifts. They present six steps of effective fundraising.

Kulp, Ann Z. *Spirit Windows: A Handbook of Spiritual Growth Resources for Leaders*. Louisville: Bridge Resources, 1998.

> *Spirit Windows* offers many resources and practical ideas for persons who lead contemplative or intercessory prayer gatherings, meditation groups, retreats, or other events that seek to enhance participants' awareness of God. Woven throughout the book are suggestions for using breathing, physical relaxation, imaging, journaling, chanting, music, Scripture, and worship as aids to spiritual awareness.

McCormick, Gwenn E. *Planning and Building Church Facilities*. Nashville: Broadman, 1992.

> Produced within the Baptist tradition, this book is a comprehensive guide to the building process. Special attention is given to organizing committees, paying attention to property and financial issues, working with an architect, and attending to accessibility issues. Relatively little is said about the function of worship and the ways that worship will shape the space, but the advice on process is helpful.

Melander, Rochelle, and Harold Eppley. *Growing Together: Spiritual Exercises for Church Committees*. Minneapolis: Augsburg, 1998.

> This book contains fifty exercises that congregational groups can use to build community and encourage spiritual growth. The exercises are designed to take fifteen to twenty minutes and include an opening prayer, a time for sharing, a biblical reflection period, and a closing prayer.

Messner, Roe. *Church Growth by Design: A Complete Guide for Planning and Building Churches to God's Glory*. Matthews, NC: Empire Group, 2003.

> Messner offers logical steps and the wisdom of experience in this guide. The first seven chapters cover preliminaries of decision making in terms of determining feasibility, planning finances, selecting the site, forming building committees, and choosing architects and builders. The remaining eleven chapters address in detail all aspects of designing the facility, inside and out.

Olsen, Charles M. *Transforming Church Boards into Communities of Spiritual Leaders*. Herndon, VA: Alban, 1995.

> Based on his extensive experience with church boards, Olsen presents practical suggestions for how boards may become spiritual leaders. At the heart of vision is the proposal that a board meeting should more closely resemble a worship service than a business council; hymn singing, prayers, biblical reflection, and storytelling should be the norm. What Olsen describes for board meetings can be applicable to congregational building committees as well.

Oswald, Roy M., and Robert E. Friedrich Jr. *Discerning Your Congregation's Future: A Strategic and Spiritual Approach*. Herndon, VA: Alban, 1996.

A step-by-step guide to congregational planning that grounds strategic planning techniques in a process of spiritual discernment. The result: members will own the vision and be eager to participate in the congregation's calling, life, and ministry.

Partners for Sacred Places
1700 Sansom St., Tenth Floor
Philadelphia, PA 19103
215-567-3234; FAX 215-567-3235
partners@sacredplaces.org
www.sacredplaces.org

Partners for Sacred Places is a nonprofit organization devoted to helping Americans care for and make good use of older and historic religious properties. Partners maintains an information clearinghouse, accessible from its Web site, which contains extensive building-related resources. Partners also publishes resources related to property maintenance and fundraising.

Percept
29889 Santa Margarita Parkway
Rancho Santa Margarita, CA 92688-3609
800-442-6277 or 949-635-3609
FAX 949-635-1283
http://www.percept1.com/pacific/start.asp

Percept is a strategic information company that offers demographic products and other planning resources to help churches, judicatories, and parachurch organizations engage in mission.

Project Delivery System Selection Workbook. Austin, TX: Construction Industry Institute, 1999.

> This resource was published by the Construction Industry Institute to help owners select an appropriate project delivery system. The workbook includes a six-step selection tool designed to help owners select from one of three principle project delivery systems used in the United States—the traditional design-bid-build, design-build, and construction management at risk.

Rejoice in Your Handiwork: Sacred Space and Synagogue Architecture. Part 1: Congregational Guide to the Process of Renovating and Building; Part 2: Form and Function: Design Considerations for Congregations. New York: Union for Reform Judaism, 2005.

> This two-part free downloadable resource available from the Union of Reform Judaism Web site, www.urj.org, provides a comprehensive guide for congregations planning to build or expand synagogues. Drawing on the experience of synagogues that have firsthand knowledge of building projects, the Union of Reform Judaism has produced a resource that covers the major aspects of building. Part 1 focuses on land use, relocation, maintenance and repair, forming teams within the congregation, selecting architects and contractors, funding, and much more. The appendix for part 1 includes very practical checklists and guides for aspects of congregational building projects, such as a form to use for assessing space use. Part 2 of this resource relates to issues such as creating intimacy, sensory experiences, and so forth. The appendix in part 2 includes a four-session study guide for group discussion of congregational space based on sacred texts. Although written for Reform Jews, congregations of all faith traditions will find a lot of useful information in this resource.

Rendle, Gil, and Alice Mann. *Holy Conversations: Strategic Planning as a Spiritual Practice for Congregations*. Herndon, VA: Alban, 2003.

> Gil Rendle and Alice Mann describe a "holy conversation" as a congregational discernment process that centers on three critical questions: Who are we? What has God called us to do or be? Who is our neighbor?

Sanvido, Victor, and Mark Konchar. *Selecting Project Delivery Systems: Comparing Design-Build, Design-Bid-Build and Construction Management at Risk*. State College, PA: The Project Delivery Institute, 1999.

> How might a major study of project delivery systems help a congregation make informed choices? The answer lies in this handbook of objective data obtained from results of the U.S. Project Delivery System Study. It contains concise summaries of results and procedures in a format for quick comprehension. Chapters contain easily understandable charts, graphs, bullet points, and a "Thoughts for the Reader" section. It begins by defining the systems studied and highlighting the results. Questions are then posed to help the facility owner select an appropriate delivery system. A comprehensive outline is given to help identify needs and goals to generate a profile of the organization. Guidance is offered for selecting and implementing a project delivery system. Finally, the book highlights success factors found as a result of this study. This source could provide building committees with real data and practical suggestions for choosing the best system for their building needs.

Skjegstad, Joy. *Winning Grants to Strengthen Your Ministry*. Herndon, VA: Alban Institute, 2007.

> Skjegstad is an experienced grant-proposal writer who has successfully raised money for a variety of nonprofits over the past twenty years. She shows how fundraising can be an integral part of ministry and provides detailed guidance on the practical aspects of seeking grants from foundation and corporate funders.

Smith, Peter E. *Cherubim of Gold: Building Materials and Aesthetics*. Meeting House Essays, no. 3. Chicago, IL: Liturgy Training Publications, 1993.

> Smith argues that prefabricated, functional materials used for church structures robs the congregants of the mystery and awe that are prompted by use of natural materials such as marble, limestone, brick, terra-cotta, and oak.

TAG
Kevin Ford, Chief Visionary Officer
3541 Chain Bridge Rd., Suite 6
Fairfax, VA 22030
877-824-5463; FAX 703-385-9621
kford@877tagline.com

> TAG is a consulting organization that can assist congregations with internal and external assessment, strategic planning, and coaching. TAG conducts community needs studies, market research, and demographic studies.

Traditional Building: The Professional's Resource for Public Architecture, 16, no. 6 (November–December 2003).

Traditional Building is a bi-monthly publication for professionals in architecture, interior design, construction, and landscape design. This issue is the annual publication devoted to religious buildings. It contains supplier lists in such areas as stone carvings; slate, tile and metal roofing; steeples; art glass; interior lighting; and many more.

Transforming Church Index
TAG (see page 245)

The Transforming Church Index is a survey of church members that assesses a congregation's capacity for healthy growth. Some areas covered in the survey include communications, outreach, leadership, member satisfaction, and assimilation. Results of the survey are compared with national norms from congregations of all sizes, locations, and denominations.

U.S. Census
www.census.gov

A wealth of information about your congregation's community can be gleaned from the U.S. Census Web site. This information includes age, race, economic and education characteristics, and much more for your neighborhood. In addition, population projections are provided, based on the 2000 census.

The U.S. Congregational Life Survey
http://www.uscongregations.org

> U.S. Congregations, a religious research group, developed the U.S. Congregational Life Survey to enable congregations to identify and build on their strengths. The research-based survey enables congregations to compare their strengths to national and denominational benchmarks. U.S. Congregations provides an array of resources to help congregations maximize the strengths they identify in the survey.

Vassallo, Wanda. *Church Communications Handbook: A Complete Guide to Developing a Strategy, Using Technology, Writing Effectively, and Reaching the Unchurched.* Grand Rapids: Kregel, 1998.

> This resource is a comprehensive reference book for congregational communications. Two chapters are particularly apropos for congregations going through a sacred space process. Chapter 10: "Taking the Pulse of Your Congregation," suggests ways to get input from members of the congregation, including focus groups and questionnaires. Chapter 11, "On the Move to a New Location," provides communication ideas for congregations that are relocating.

Vision and the Church
www.congregationalresources.org/LearningPathway/
VnCWelcome.asp

> Vision and the Church is an interactive online learning experience designed to be used by congregations desiring to discover or reaffirm their vision.

Vosko, Richard S. *Designing Future Worship Spaces*. Meeting House Essays, no. 8. Chicago: Liturgy Training Publications, 1996.

> Vosko explores the dissatisfaction with the "new look" of contemporary Roman Catholic churches that often focus on functionality instead of art. He notes that contemporary trends in church architecture are influenced by cultural dynamics, including changing religious attitudes. The author argues that church buildings should be places of beauty, justice, imagination, and memory.

"You and Your Architect"
www.aia.org/consumer/news/YouandYourArchitect.pdf

> "You and Your Architect" is a free downloadable article available from the Web site of the American Institute of Architects. The article includes a helpful chart of the services architects can provide. It also addresses selecting an architect, negotiating the agreement, compensating the architect, and keeping the project on track.

Your Sacred Place Is a Community Asset: A Tool Kit to Attract New Resources and Partners. Philadelphia: Partners for Sacred Places, 2002.

> Partners for Sacred Places has developed this resource to help congregations understand the value of the services that they provide to the community and to use that information to attract new sources of funding.

Notes

Introduction

1. To learn more about the Indianapolis Center for Congregations and the Sacred Space Initiative, from which our discern, decide, and do model and other aspects of this book's material comes, see appendix E.

2. Rudolf Schwarz, *The Church Incarnate*, trans. Cynthia Harris (Chicago: Regnery, 1958), 9–10.

Chapter 1 Who Are We as a Congregation?

1. Annie Dillard, *Teaching a Stone to Talk* (San Francisco: Harper Perennial, 1988), 85-94.

2. Genesis 31.

3. Margaret Visser, *The Geometry of Love* (New York: North Point Press, 2001).

4. Richard Taylor, *How to Read a Church: A Guide to Symbols and Images in Churches and Cathedrals* (Mahwah, NJ: Hidden Spring, 2005).

5. George Herbert, *A Priest in the Temple* (Milwaukee: Young Churchman, 1915).

Chapter 2 Who Are Our Neighbors?

1. *The American Heritage Dictionary of the English Language*, 4th ed., Dictionary.com, http://dictionary.reference.com/browse/demographics (accessed October 3, 2006).

2. Adapted from Kevin Ford, presentation to Sacred Space project directors, Indianapolis, September 2004.

3. http://factfinder.census.gov.

4. http://www.perceptnet.com.

5. www.thearda.com.

6. Ford presentation.

7. www.studycircles.org.

8. www.map.nazarene.org.

9. We realize that there are areas of study around assets, including appreciative inquiry and asset mapping. Here we are not referring to one of these models but to strengths and helpful services in a community. As you work on your building project, you will want to be aware of and understand how these "assets" affect your mission and therefore your building project.

10. Ford presentation.

11. Nancy Ammerman, *Congregation and Community* (New Brunswick, NJ: Rutgers University Press, 1999), 377-80.

12. Gil Rendle and Alice Mann, *Holy Conversations* (Herndon, VA: Alban, 2003), 113-26.

13. Ibid., 74.

Chapter 3 Who Is God Calling Us to Be?

1. Robert Norton and Richard Southern, *Cracking Your Congregation's Code: Mapping Your Spiritual DNA to Create Your Future* (San Francisco: Jossey-Bass, 2001), 24.

2. Ibid., 164.

3. Gil Rendle and Alice Mann, *Holy Conversations* (Herndon, VA: Alban, 2003), 84.

4. Norton and Southern, *Cracking Your Congregation's Code*, 167.

5. www.transformingchurchindex.com.

6. For more information, see their Web site at www.uscongregations. org.

7. Kevin Ford, presentation to Sacred Space project directors, Indianapolis, September 2004.

8. Rendle and Mann, *Holy Conversations*, 84.

9. For more information about the pre-mortem exercise, see Gary Klein, *Sources of Power* (Boston: MIT Press, 1999), 71-72.

Chapter 4 What Do We Want Our Building to Convey?

1. Martin Marty and Micah Marty, *Our Hope for Years to Come* (Minneapolis: Fortress, 1995).

2. David Spero, *Churches* (London: SteidlMACK, 2006) and Camilo José Vergara, *How the Other Half Worships* (New Brunswick, NJ: Rutgers University Press, 2005).

3. Edward Farley, *Faith and Beauty: A Theological Aesthetic* (Burlington, VT: Ashgate, 2001), 45-46.

4. Jim Croegaert, "Why Do We Hunger for Beauty?" Meadowgreen Music/Heart of the Matter Music, copyright 1989.

5. Frank Burch Brown, *Good Taste, Bad Taste and Christian Taste: Aesthetics in Religious Life* (New York: Oxford Press, 2000), 251.

6. Michael Rose, *Ugly as Sin: Why They Changed Our Churches from Sacred Places to Meeting Spaces and How We Can Change Them Back Again* (Manchester, NH: Sophia Institute Press, 2001).

7. Brown, *Good Taste, Bad Taste and Christian Taste*, 251. This is good advice for people working together on aesthetics.

8. Gretchen T. Buggein, "Sacred Spaces: Designing America's Churches," *Christian Century*, June 2004, 20-25.

9. Ray Oldenburg, *The Great Good Place: Cafes, Coffee Shops, Bookstores, Bars, Hair Salons, and Other Hangouts at the Heart of a Community* (Berkeley, CA: Marlowe, 1999).

10. Richard Vosko, in introduction to Michael Crosbie, *Architecture for the Gods* (New York: Watson-Gutptill, 2000), 9.

Chapter 5 What Approach to Building Will We Use?

1. Bill Chegwidden, *The Next Step: How to Discover the Right Solutions to Plan, Design, and Build Your Church* (Canton, GA: Riverstone Group, 2004), 207-15.

2. AIA California Council, *Handbook on Project Delivery* (Sacramento: American Institute of Architects, California Council, 1996).

3. Chegwidden actually uses the term "negotiated bid contract." We have chosen to use the term "negotiated select team" to focus on the "team" aspect of this approach.

4. Victor Sanvido and Mark Konchar, *Selecting Project Delivery Systems: Comparing Design-Build, Design-Bid-Build and Construction Management at Risk* (State College, PA: The Project Delivery Institute, 1999), 2.

5. Chegwidden, *Next Step*, 211.

6. Ibid.

7. Ibid., 224.

8. AIA California Council, *Handbook on Project Delivery*.

9. Sanvido and Konchar, *Selecting Project Delivery Systems*, 3.

Chapter 6 What Service Providers Will We Use?

1. *Sacred Space: Discern, Decide, Do* (Indianapolis: Indianapolis Center for Congregations, 2005). DVD.

2. *Built of Living Stones: Art, Architecture, and Worship* (Washington, DC: United States Conference of Catholic Bishops, 2000).

3. *Rejoice in Your Handiwork: Sacred Space and Synagogue Architecture* is a two-part, free, downloadable resource available at http://urj. org/synmgmt/publications/.

4. Available at the Church Extension Web site: www. churchextension.org.

5. Available at the Baptist General Conference of Texas Web site: http://www.bgct.org/texasbaptists/Page. aspx?&pid=656&srcid=236.

6. Bill Chegwidden, *The Next Step: How to Discover the Right Solutions to Plan, Design, and Build Your Church* (Canton, GA: Riverstone Group, 1996).

7. *Beyond Reading: Using Books as Resources*, Using Resources Series (Indianapolis: Indianapolis Center for Congregations). Available on the Center's Web site: www.centerforcongregations.org.

8. See for example, the American Institute of Architects, www. aia.org, and National Association of Church Design-Builders, www. nacdb.com.

9. The American Institute of Architects Web site, www.aia.org, also provides a variety of resources related to architects and their services, including a helpful free online article titled "You and Your Architect." Congregations exploring the design-build model will want to consult the following organizations: The Design-Build Institute of America (DBA) at www.dbia and the National Association of Church Design Builders at www.nacdb.org.

10. The Associated General Contractors of America is the trade association for the construction industry. Contact them at The Associated General Contractors of America, 2300 Wilson Blvd., Suite 400, Arlington, VA 22201, 703-548-3118, www.agc.org.

11. "Hiring a Contractor: What You Should Know," Brotherhood Mutual Insurance Company Article Archive, www.brotherhoodmutual.

com/NAV-pages/43-HiringAContractor.shtml. Contact them at Brotherhood Mutual Insurance Company, 6400 Brotherhood Way, Fort Wayne, IN 46825, 800-333-3735, www.brotherhoodmutual. com.

12. Baptist Builders—A Ministry of the North American Mission Board, Southern Baptist Conference, www.namb.net, 800-462-8647.

13. Laborers for Christ, Lutheran Church–Missouri Synod. Visit the denomination's Web site, www.lcms.org, and use the search feature to find Laborers for Christ.

14. Cooperative Baptist Fellowship. P.O. Box 450329, Atlanta, GA 31145, 770-220-1600, wwwthefellowship.info.

15. Marilyn McClellan, "Over 300 Volunteers Pitch in to Construct New UCC Church." Free online article available at the United Church of Christ's Web site, www.ucc.org/ucnews/mar04/construct.htm.

Chapter 7 What Sources of Funding Will We Use?

1. Jerry Cripps, "Developing Successful Congregational Building Projects," Sacred Space Presentation, Indianapolis, 2004.

2. Means QuickCost Estimator, www.rsmeans.com/calculator/index.asp; McGraw Hill Commercial Construction Cost Estimator, http://costest.construction.com/cest/.

3. Church Extension, Christian Church (Disciples of Christ), www.churchextension.org.

4. Baptist General Conference of Texas, http://www.bgct.org/texasbaptists/Page.aspx?&pid=656&srcid=236.

5. Bill Chegwidden, *The Next Step: How to Discover the Right Solutions to Plan, Design, and Build Your Church* (Canton, GA: Riverstone Group, 2004), 122-34.

6. Gwenn E. McCormick, *Planning and Building Church Facilities* (Nashville: Broadman, 1992), 72; Patrick L. Clements, *Proven Concepts of Church Building and Finance: A Step-by-Step Guide to Successful Building Projects* (Grand Rapids: Kregel, 2002), 75; Jerry Cripps, "Developing Successful Congregational Building Projects."

7. Chegwidden, *The Next Step*, 162.

8. Clements, *Proven Concepts of Church Building and Finance*, 86.

9. Chegwidden, *The Next Step*, 162.

10. Church Extension, Christian Church (Disciples of Christ), www.churchextension.org.

11. Partners for Sacred Places, 1700 Sansom Street, Tenth Floor, Philadelphia, PA 19103, 215-567-3234, www.sacredplaces.org.

12. Partners for Sacred Places. *Your Sacred Place Is a Community Asset: A Tool Kit to Attract New Resources and Partners* (Philadelphia: Partners for Sacred Places, 2002).

13. Glenn N. Holliman and Barbara L. Holliman, *With Generous Hearts: How to Gather Resources for Your Church, Church School, Church Agency, Chaplaincy or Diocese*, rev. ed. (Harrisburg, PA: Morehouse, 2005).

14. Association of Fundraising Professionals, 101 King Street, Suite 700, Alexandria, VA, 22314, 703-684-0410, www.afpnet. org.

15. "Selecting Fundraising Consultants," Using Resources Series (Indianapolis: Indianapolis Center for Congregations, 2004).

16. *Congregational Stories: Fund Drive*. Congregational Stories Series (Indianapolis: Indianapolis Center for Congregations, n.d.).

17. Peggy Powell Dean and Susanna A. Jones, *The Complete Guide to Capital Campaigns for Historic Churches and Synagogues*, rev. ed. (Philadelphia: Partners for Sacred Places, 1998), 13.

18. Donald W. Joiner and Norma Wimberly, *The Abington Guide to Funding Ministry*, vol. 3 (Nashville: Abingdon, 1997), 116-22.

Chapter 8 How Will We Keep the Congregation Informed?

1. Kennon L. Callahan, *Building for Effective Mission: A Complete Guide for Congregations on Bricks and Mortar Issues* (San Francisco: Jossey-Bass, 1995), 102-4.

Chapter 9 How Will We Maintain Our Spiritual Focus?

1. Danny Morris and Charles Olsen, *Discerning God's Will Together: A Spiritual Practice for the Church* (Herndon, VA: Alban, 1997), 65-93.

2. See www.renovare.com, www.upperroom.com, www.purposedriven.com, www.wholecommunitycatechesis.com.

3. Jon Pahl, *Shopping Malls and Other Sacred Spaces: Putting God in Place* (Grand Rapids: Brazos, 2003), 65-82.

4. Ibid. For a full discussion of the metaphors, see 123-27, 139-258.

5. Jon Pahl presentation to Sacred Space project directors, Indianapolis, September 2004.

Chapter 10 How Will We Ensure That the Work Is Done Properly?

1. *Taking a Closer Look: Using Facilities Assessments*, Using Resources Series (Indianapolis: The Indianapolis Center for Congregations, 2006).

2. Kennon Callahan, *Building for Effective Mission: A Complete Guide for Congregations on Bricks and Mortar Issues* (San Francisco: Jossey-Bass, 1995), 103.

3. "Guidance for Engineers Performing Site Observation Services," National Society of Professional Engineers, http://www. nspe.org/liability/in-home.asp.

4. Appendix D, "Characteristics of Effective Owners' Representatives," in *Progress in Improving Project Management at the Department of Energy: 2002 Assessment* (National Research Council, 2003), 92-95.

5. A Web site helpful for finding a local inspector in your region is http://inspectorlinks.com/property_inspector_index.htm.

Appendix E Sacred Space Grants Initiative

1. These partners include Kevin Ford of TAG, Bob Jaeger and Tuomi Forrest of Partners for Sacred Places, and architect Jerry Cripps of InterDesign.